# FIELD GUIDE TO NEGOTIATION

HARVARD BUSINESS / THE ECONOMIST REFERENCE SERIES

**Field Guide to Business Terms:** *A Glossary of Essential Tools and Concepts for Today's Manager*

**Field Guide to Marketing Terms:** *A Glossary of Essential Tools and Concepts for Today's Manager*

**Field Guide to Strategy:** *A Glossary of Essential Tools and Concepts for Today's Manager*

**Field Guide to Negotiation:** *A Glossary of Essential Tools and Concepts for Today's Manager*

# FIELD GUIDE TO NEGOTIATION:

## *A Glossary of Essential Tools and Concepts for Today's Manager*

**Gavin Kennedy**

*Boston, Massachusetts*

Published in the United States by Harvard Business School Press
Copyright © 1994 by The Economist Books Ltd.

Printed in the United States of America

98  97  96  95  94       5  4  3  2  1 (pbk)

98  97  96  95  94       5  4  3  2  1 (hard)

*Field Guide to Negotiation* is part of the Harvard Business/
The Economist Reference Book Series and is based on
material first published in Great Britain in 1993 by The
Economist Books Ltd.

The paper used in this publication meets the requirements
of the American National Standard for Permanence of Paper
for Printed Library Materials Z39.49-1984.

Library of Congress Cataloging-in-Publication Data

Kennedy, Gavin.
    Field guide to negotiation : a glossary of essential tools
and concepts for today's manager / Gavin Kennedy.
        p.  cm. — (Harvard Business/The Economist
    reference series)
    ISBN 0-87584-480-4 (hc) — ISBN 0-87584-481-2 (pb)
    1. Negotiation in business.  2. Negotiation—
Terminology.
I. Title.  II. Series.
HD58.6.K463  1994
658.4—dc20                                        93-39920
                                                      CIP

*Series design by Mike Fender*

# CONTENTS

# PREFACE

*Field Guide to Negotiation* helps you understand and manage the process of negotiation. It is meant to be consulted more than once, dipped into and thought about before, or even during, your negotiations.

The guide is an *aide memoire,* not a treatise. It suggests insights rather than elaborate concepts. It is full of practical tips. It also explains some academic theories without neglecting the real world of business negotiation. *Field Guide to Negotiation* is not a tool for bluffing your way through a negotiation. Its approach is not Machiavellian. Bluffs are usually counterproductive and best left to unserious amateurs and armchair voyeurs of the real world of business.

When manipulative ploys are identified, the aim is to prepare you for what might come across the table rather than to arm you with tricks to trap the other negotiators. A ploy identified is a ploy neutralized. *Field Guide to Negotiation* is a practical as well as an informative guide to negotiating.

Many people have influenced my work on negotiation in the past 22 years—too many to mention here—and I hope they will forgive me for not fully acknowledging my numerous debts to them. I have space to make only one exception, namely my colleague and friend, Colin Rose, in Victoria, Australia. In two areas in particular Colin has contributed much to my thinking and practice: first on the different styles of negotiation, and second on seeing the three phases of negotiation from the perspective of parties seeking what they want. The former is summarized in the opening essay on handling difficult negotiators (although Colin may enter a disclaimer to my interpretation and presentation).

Gavin Kennedy

# INTRODUCTION

We often find ourselves in conflict with others: customers who want it yesterday, rivals who can supply it today, suppliers who will not deliver to our deadlines (and certainly not when they promised), customers who claim that they never received what we dispatched a week ago, colleagues who cannot see us when we need them and cannot see what we know is in their best interests, employees who want more pay (and time off), families who spend it before we earn it, children who think we are a bottomless pit, and bosses who think they know whose fault it is.

We negotiate to find acceptable solutions to these and other conflicts. We start with two solutions (yours and mine) to the same problem: two prices, two shares, two delivery dates, two wage rates, two specifications, two times to meet, two budget levels, two amounts of pocket money. When we negotiate, we search for one solution with which both can agree. It is unlikely to be the solution that either of us started with; if it were, then somebody would have given in, which is not a negotiation.

We all have considerable negotiation experience. We

become adults after a long apprenticeship in negotiation: from the number of peas we must eat before we get some ice cream (our first negotiations are in the kitchen, not the boardroom), to the reward we receive for tidying our room, to whom we can play with and where, to what we can watch on television. As teenagers we negotiate part of our courtship ritual, including "your place or mine?".

By the time we start our first jobs we are ready for the constant negotiation over the allocation of resources.

Mostly we do not think about negotiation, any more than we think about its alternatives such as persuasion, giving in, instruction, haggling, coercion, and joint problem solving. We switch into and out of negotiation without thinking, sometimes getting what we want and sometimes not. Yet if we tap the rich seam of our own experience, apply some obvious but often-forgotten techniques, and begin to think about what we normally do without thought, we can improve our negotiating performance dramatically.

That is the main purpose of *Field Guide to Negotiation:* to improve your performance as a negotiator. To help you achieve this result, four short essays precede the glossary. The selection of essay topics was based on my experience with the questions most commonly asked at seminars. We do not suggest that they are comprehensive, but we present them on the premise that if negotiators continually ask these questions, there is a benefit in including them in a book designed to be kept close by.

# PART 1

# *ESSAYS*

## WHAT IS THE BASIS FOR THE DIFFERENT STYLES OF NEGOTIATION?

Negotiation is about trading. This distinguishes it from other forms of decision making. In negotiation there is an explicit trade: I get some of what I want, and you get some of what you want. We trade what we have that others want for what we want from them.

We do not, however, negotiate in a contextual vacuum. Because we happen to be meeting to make a decision, it does not follow necessarily that either of us attempts to make explicit trades. Each can seek to resolve the matter by various means, including trying to force the other to capitulate. Nor need we abide by any notion of "fairness." Indeed, I can attempt to exploit you with silver-tongued sales techniques, or by playing on your ignorance, or by threatening you with dire consequences if you resist my demands.

Where does this leave the party who wants to trade to arrive at a solution when the other party does not?

To evaluate the problem, consider the style dimension, divided between those who want something for nothing (Red stylists) and those who are willing to trade something for something (Blue stylists). Think of the style dimension as a continuum, with extreme Red stylists at one end and extreme Blue stylists at the other. Between the extremes are varying shades of redness, purple, and blueness.

Red stylists are characterized by their beliefs about how decisions can be made to work for them. They

- see all negotiations as one-time-only contests;
- seek to win by domination;
- believe that more for them inevitably means less for you (but that is your problem, not theirs);
- are prone to bluffs, ploys, "dirty tricks," even coercion;
- want something for nothing.

  By contrast, Blue stylists

- see any negotiation in its long-term context;
- seek to succeed by cooperation;
- believe more for you means more for them (a gain for both of you);
- eschew manipulative techniques, preferring instead to address each party's interests using negotiable tradables;
- will only trade something for something.

In practice, the clash between Red and Blue styles leads to varying outcomes. Sometimes the Blue stylist is intimidated into submission by an overtly aggressive display by the Red stylist; sometimes the Red stylist achieves the same result (something for nothing) by stealth and by hiding his or her Red intentions.

This creates the following matrix.

| **Red** | **Blue** |
|---|---|
| Aggressive | Submissive |
| Takes something for nothing | Gives something for nothing |
| Covert | Assertive |
| Finesses something for nothing | Trades something for something |

You can think of individuals who predominantly display one of the characteristics shown in the matrix. Alternatively, and more revealingly perhaps, try to think of occasions when you have displayed all four style variants.

- Any time you make an unconditional offer, you are a submissive Blue.

- Whenever you make a unilateral demand, with no offer of anything in return, you are an aggressive Red.

- On those occasions when you exploit somebody because you cannot resist the temptation, you are a covert Red.

- When you negotiate with only conditional proposals ("if you, then I, . . ."), you are an assertive Blue.

## HOW SHOULD WE HANDLE DIFFICULT NEGOTIATORS?

All the individuals we negotiate with are difficult to some degree; they do not agree with us for a start and insist on being less than enthusiastic about what we want. By difficult negotiators we mean people who behave in an extremely difficult fashion, usually aggressive Red stylists with manners (or lack thereof) to match. You know them when you deal with them, and the question is how you should handle them in a decision-making context.

That, of course, is the problem. You have come to negotiate, and they have not. Their version of a solution requires you to give them what they want (all of it) and go home quietly.

Many inexperienced decision makers behave aggressively because they confuse aggression with toughness. They adopt aggressive behavior to get what they want; because some people submit to them, they find aggression works and so they adopt it whenever they want something.

You must break the connection between intimidation and winning. If you do not, you join the submissive Blues who reinforce aggressiveness by rewarding it.

Your first action in dealing with difficult negotiators is to seize their attention so you can assert unambiguously that there are only two ways they are going to get what they want — through the merits of their case or through trading — and that you will not submit to intimidation, bullying, or threats. Second, you have the choice of matching or contrasting their style.

Style matching is risky because it responds in kind to difficult negotiators' behavior and "who started it" can easily get lost in a fog of insults and threats. It can work, however, if carefully controlled. For example, a bitter strike may have to be fought out to the finish (or look as if it is going to be) to bring the strikers to their senses and back to the negotiating table. Of course this could go horribly wrong, particularly if the strike (or terrorism, for another example) becomes the primary issue, eclipsing the merits of the case or the principle of trading.

The purpose of style matching is to avoid constructive submission and to open up an alternative route to a settlement.

Style contrast is also risky because the contrast in styles could be read by difficult negotiators as constructive submission. In other words, they might perceive that you are submitting in all but name. Instead of responding in kind to their outrageous behavior, try the following:

- Speak more quietly than they do.
- Speak more slowly than they do.
- Give way to their interruptions, but pause for a few seconds each time they finish.
- Do not respond in kind if they swear.
- Do not argue with their attacks on you and their apportioning of blame.
- Do not defend yourself against ascribed motives.
- Ignore all threats.
- Respond positively but specifically and without rancor to any Blue moves they make, even in the midst of their Red-dominated activities.
- Respond not at all to their Red moves, other than to say "no."
- Affirm whenever appropriate the two principles on which you will agree to a solution (merits of the case and trading).

Your assertive Blue message will eventually get through (see the glossary entry under SKINNER'S PIGEON).

- Toughness is not a synonym for shouting abuse, threatening, and intimidation.
- Toughness is based on an absolute and patient firmness of purpose.

## HOW DO WE DEAL WITH COVERT RED NEGOTIATORS?

The answer is: not without difficulty. The problem is that most covert Red negotiators do not start off with the intention of cheating you (some do, of course). The majority simply find it impossible to resist the temptation to do so. The opportunity to cheat creeps up on them without warning and faced with a safe "steal," they cannot resist.

The covert Red and the assertive Blue are easily confused. The fact is that you do not know whether negotiators are going to exploit you if they are themselves unaware of how they will react if the opportunity to exploit you arises. This puts you at a disadvantage, but it is one you cannot avoid. You do not know for sure how you would react if a similar opportunity arose; everyone has the potential to become covert Red in certain circumstances.

Hence you could be dealing with apparently assertive Blue negotiators, characterized by

- a cool but firm tone,
- respectful negotiating manners,
- patience in respect to the pace of your negotiation,
- an analytical rather than emotional approach, and
- demonstrable listening skills.

In short, they are behaving just as you are.

These negotiators may intend to exploit you but their behavior gives you no clues because their intentions are deliberately hidden from you (that is why they are covert). They may have no intention of cheating but cannot help it when the opportunity arises, perhaps on this single occasion. Their behavior up to that moment is genuine but they switch to the covert Red role without revealing what they have done.

If you think that you are dealing with other assertive Blues, you expose yourself to exploitation by revealing your expectations — even your interests — believing that it is safe to do so with these people (who clearly are not aggressive Red stylists). You carelessly offer movement on the implicit understanding that they will reciprocate; after all, you assume, they know it is a negotiation to be settled on the basis of trading, not conceding. You reveal something and then they strike.

- *Revelation:* You desperately require their services. *Action:* They increase their entry price and charge for add-ons when you accept it.
- *Revelation:* Your budget is in surplus with no carry-over provisions to the next quarter. *Action:* They quote a premium price despite your early payment.
- *Revelation:* You are in trouble with your cash flow. *Action:* They insist on advance payment.

Most proposals from covert Reds are willingly accepted by their victims; it is so easy to switch to the role of submissive Blue. So how do you handle them? Basically by never slipping out of the assertive Blue role, which insists that everything is traded — not conceded.

First, you must use Blue signals to test for covert Red intentions. A signal addresses the major strategic question of all negotiators: how to indicate a willingness to move without giving in. By a shift in emphasis from the affirmative defense of an opening position to a tentative willingness to consider moving, a signal indicates

that movement is possible, providing it is not interpreted as your giving in.

- From demanding full compensation, you signal that
  you require *some* compensation.
- From rejecting a demand as impossible, you signal
  that it would be contrary to normal policy.
- From rejecting a general application of a principle,
  you signal a willingness to discuss specific instances
  where it might be applicable.

The key is in how the other negotiators respond to
your signal: if they trash it, you have revealed Red stylists; if they respond positively, they might be covert
Red. And that is how it must remain. No matter what
they appear to be, you will never know whether they
are genuinely assertive Blue or potentially covert Red.

But all is not beyond hope of resolution. It depends
on what you do next. You must now consider how you
make your proposals.

Every negotiator has a Red side. If somebody offers
us what we want for nothing, we will surely take it.

- Suppose we make a proposal that consists only of a
  condition (that states what we want). What is the
  nature of this proposal? Surely, it is an aggressive Red
  stylist's attempt to get something for nothing.
- Suppose we make a proposal that consists only of an
  offer (that gives the other party what it wants). What
  is the nature of this proposal? Surely it is a submissive Blue stylist's free concession, giving something
  away for nothing.

Thus these two proposals by themselves are the currency of either the aggressive Red or the submissive Blue
stylist. They are like the two elements sodium and chlo-

rine, which are poisonous to humans if ingested separately but are the foundation of life (salt) when ingested together.

The assertive Blue negotiator is in an analogous situation. Separately, the condition and the offer are the antithesis of decision by negotiation; together, they constitute the very essence of what negotiation is about. Combine them into a conditional proposal and the assertive negotiator is totally protected whatever the style coming across the table, overt or covert.

| Condition | Offer |
|---|---|
| Your Red side stating | Your Blue side stating |
| what you want | what they want |

"If you give me what I want . . . then I will give you what you want."

You can think of the conditional proposal as a purple style (a bit of Red and a bit of Blue, the proportions depending on the terms you are attempting to strike for a deal).

Conditional proposals consisting of your Red conditions and your Blue offers are purple defenses against any Red plays, whether openly aggressive or covertly snatched. Conditionality asserts that they cannot get what they want from you without you getting what you want from them.

The conditional proposal has several potential effects:

- It stumps the aggressive Red stylist to the extent that you mean it.
- It poses no threat to the submissive Blues because they are too used to giving things away for nothing.

This way they get something back. (You never meant to exploit them, did you?)

- It flummoxes the covert Reds, because to challenge the trading principle they would have to reveal their Red intentions; and by definition, the covert cannot do that.
- It is no problem at all for genuine assertive Blues because they apply the trading principle themselves in all of their dealings.

## WHAT IS THE ROLE OF MANIPULATIVE PLOYS?

There is a considerable market in offering so-called streetwise advice on negotiating. To a lot of people, negotiation is about dirty tricks, ploys, gambits, and so-called tactics, and they are prepared to pay good money to hear about it.

Unfortunately, much of this advice is unhelpful. It is true that learning about the manipulative approach has value to the extent that in conducting regular business negotiation you will be the object of numerous attempted tactical ploys. Because negotiation is an unscripted interaction with no absolute rules, no appeals, and no comebacks, it may appear on the surface that the manipulative approach is dominant and the one you must become adept at quickly if you are to do well.

Knowledge of manipulative approaches is dangerous, however, if you confuse identifying what some people might try to do to you in a negotiation with what you must learn to do to others. Courses that teach tactical manipulation often fail to account for the fact that in a real negotiation you might forget the appropriate ploy for the situation or apply the wrong ploy for the situation.

In the glossary we identify numerous ploys and tricks, but here we emphasize the difference between introducing manipulative tactics that may be used against you and encouraging you to become manipulative. A ploy identified by you in the course of a negotiating exchange is a ploy neutralized. Moreover, if you know that the negotiators are attempting to manipulate you, it should alert you to their Red intentions.

All ploys, tricks, and bluffs have a single aim: to influence your perception of the power of your partner in negotiation. Why? Because perceptions of power and your expectations are linked.

• The less power you perceive them to have relative to you, the higher your expectation of the outcome.

• The more power you perceive them to have relative to you, the lower your expectation of the outcome.

Therefore manipulative negotiators have a strong incentive to work on your perceptions of their power. It directly influences what you expect to result from the negotiation.

If you perceive your power to be

• nonexistent in the situation, you are likely to give up;

• negligible in the situation, you are likely to give in;

• balanced with theirs, you are likely to trade;

• overwhelming, you are likely to impose compliance.

All manipulative ploys can be divided into three main phases in a negotiation, depending on their tactical roles.

**1.** Dominance

**2.** Shaping

**3.** Closing

In phase 1, manipulators work to dominate you and the proceedings. They might initiate any combination of the following:

- Insist on preconditions
- Declare some issues nonnegotiable
- Attempt to decide the agenda, its order, and the timing unilaterally
- Behave in an aggressive Red style
- Hint at threats of sanctions
- Disdainfully dismiss you, your products, your business, and your views

In phase 2, manipulators work to shape the deal in their favor. They might do one of the following:

- Play good cop/bad cop
- Use add-on
- Try Mother Hubbard
- Try Russian Front

In phase 3, manipulators work to close the deal on their terms. Here are some things they might do:

- Demand you split the difference
- Claim it is "now or never"
- Set a phony deadline
- Threaten with the "or else" close
- Bluff a walk-out.

By identifying the likely ploys (and there are many more than those we have just cited) you can win the battle to influence your perceptions.

If you understand how manipulators behave, you will find it easier to counter their ploys (every ploy has a counter) or to ignore them (any ignored ploy is weakened).

If your perceptions are uninfluenced by the manipulators, you can concentrate on negotiating the issues.

# PART 2

# *GLOSSARY*

### ADD-ON

A ploy to increase the quoted terms for a transaction. The add-on is a plausible extra such as delivery or fitting or some necessary component (batteries, wires, plugs, and so on) added to the cost of the main item.

The technique is to quote basic prices only and then add on for ancillaries, or divide your product or service into component parts and set prices for the main components and add-on prices for the rest.

*Counter:* Find out what you get for your money before you give a BUYING SIGNAL.

### ADJOURNMENT

The negotiator's equivalent of a time-out. You agree to terminate the current negotiating session and adjourn for a while. This may be minutes in the corridor, hours in another room, or days back at your own site. You need a break to do one or more of the following:

• Think about what has been said

• Reconsider your position

• Regroup your team

• Consult with your advisors or more senior decision makers

• Put pressure on the other negotiators if they are anxious to come to an agreement quickly

• Rest and recuperate

Adjournments are risky because circumstances can change; for example, your rivals make irresistible proposals or even find a product better than yours.

Negotiators calling for an adjournment also create EX-PECTATIONS that they may be unable to fulfill on their return. If you do no more than restate your preadjourn-ment position, you risk creating hostility.

Always make clear why you are adjourning. If the other side calls for an adjournment, it is best to agree. Avoid "valedictory" exhortations and speeches once an adjournment is called. They waste TIME, and risk further ARGUMENT.

### ADVANCE

Payment of part (a deposit) or all of the charge for ser-vices yet to be performed. But will the services be per-formed afterward?

Avoid advance payments to people you do not know. If they are short of cash, they are unreliable. If, plausi-bly, they need money for materials, buy them yourself and deliver them to your premises, not theirs.

If a reputable business wants an advance payment (get a signed and dated receipt), require a DISCOUNT on the PRICE at least equivalent to the interest you lose while they have your money. Banks do not lend money for nothing, so why should you?

### AGENDA

An order of business. It sets out the sequence of the issues to be negotiated; it is a helpful organizer of what would otherwise be a wandering debate.

You can agree on the composition of an agenda but disagree on the order in which items will be discussed. One solution is to agree to negotiate the items in any order on the basis that "nothing is agreed until every-thing is agreed."

Extremely hostile relationships between negotiators preclude detailed agendas. But agreement to consider an agenda is a step forward, and the less specific the headings on the agenda, the more likely the parties are to agree to meet.

## AGENT

Someone who represents a PRINCIPAL to third parties. Used in real estate transactions and for the buying and selling of goods and services.

In some countries specific laws protect agents, making it difficult to terminate an agency — at least cheaply — if circumstances suggest you should do so. Many countries require foreigners to operate exclusively through nationals who act as commercial agents (see GO-BETWEEN), but some specifically prohibit the use of local agents (because of bribery scandals).

It is essential to know about local practices to avoid surprise penalties and unplanned jail sentences.

There are four important prerequisites in negotiating an agency contract.

1.  Strictly define your agent's authority and the limits to your liability.
2.  Strictly define the territory.
3.  Reserve the right to terminate the agency
    *   if sales and profit targets are not met,
    *   if payments are not made on time,
    *   if the agency is taken over by another party,
    *   if the agent is discovered to be in breach of trust, or
    *   if the agent fails to maintain declared standards of quality.

**4.** Include a dated TERMINATION clause that enables you to reassign the agency to another party, redefine the extent of the territory, renegotiate any of the terms of the agency, or take over direct distribution of your own product.

## AGREEMENT

We tend to think of a contract as a formal kind of agreement — but when arbitration leads to a settlement, the parties draw up an agreement that is formal and binding.

Record what was agreed on *while the negotiation is in progress*, not after you have dispersed. If you cannot agree on what was agreed while you are together, it is unlikely that you will do so later. If you cannot agree, continue negotiating until you can.

Record the agreement in a mutually acceptable form. All agreements should outline the action to be taken by each party to implement the agreement.

## ALTERNATIVE

If the negotiated possibilities are inferior to the available alternatives, it is better to abandon an attempt to negotiate the differences (see BATNA).

The more alternatives you have, the stronger your negotiating position.

## AMBIGUITY

May be intentional or unintentional. Intentional ambiguities arise when there is a need for a face-saving formula to break a DEADLOCK: "You interpret it your way and we will interpret it our way."

Employer-union PROCEDURE agreements state that

"The employers have the right to manage their enterprises and the unions have the right to exercise their functions." These rights overlap and, depending on the circumstances and the economic climate, one side's interpretation could trespass on the other's.

### APPLES AND ORANGES

A substitute PROPOSAL need not be comparable.

When several proposals exist it is often difficult to make accurate comparisons because each proposal varies in a different respect from the others. They are similar in that they are fruit, but one is an apple and the other is an orange.

### ARBITRATION

Use of a private tribunal or person (arbitrator) to adjudicate a dispute between parties instead of recourse to litigation.

Many countries have a legal basis for the use of arbitrators, sometimes making the arbitrator's decision legally binding on the parties (as in U.S. and Australian labor law). Sometimes it is a nonbinding, voluntary arrangement that arises out of a conciliation process (such as the United Kingdom's Advisory, Conciliation and Arbitration Service, ACAS).

If you are unable to resolve a dispute, refer the issue to a mutually acceptable third party who, for a fee, receives submissions from each side (written or oral), exercises judgment, and pronounces a verdict.

Alternatively, you and the disputing party each can nominate one person each, and the two nominees then choose a third person to form an arbitration panel. Negotiators cease to influence the outcome if their dispute goes to arbitration. Their case stands or falls on its merits as judged by the arbitrator. (See **PENDULUM ARBITRATION**)

The International Chamber of Commerce provides an arbitration service for commercial contracts (for details contact ICC Court of Arbitration, 28 Cours Albert 1 er, 75008 Paris, France).

Compare arbitration, which is usually binding, with these alternatives:

- Nonbinding arbitration. For example, a panel issues a "recommendation" of a precise finding on either the merits, the damages, or both; the parties do not have to accept the result.
- Mediation. Also nonbinding. A mediator acts as a facilitator of a process in which the parties themselves try to reach a mutually acceptable settlement.

### ARGUMENT

Argument is a destructive form of debate.

Some negotiations never get beyond argument. We can only negotiate a **PROPOSAL**. Argument prevents proposals being formulated or prevents their being considered constructively. Destructive argument is characterized by the following:

- Emotive language
- Point scoring
- Blaming, swearing, and cursing
- Attacking the other negotiator's integrity
- Questioning the other's authority
- Interrupting
- Shouting down

- Mocking
- Being generally obstructive

### ASPIRATIONS

The world is full of unfulfilled ambitions. Some research shows that high aspirations produce better results than do low aspirations; you never get more than you ask for. Other research shows high aspirations result in a higher incidence of DEADLOCK.

Balance the prize of a poor reward with the price of easily fulfilled ambition. When a party with high aspirations meets a party with low aspirations, the less ambitious party sometimes gives way: ambition becomes self-fulfilling. Alternatively, the overambitious negotiator may antagonize the less ambitious one. Worms turn; they fight back; sometimes they gain enough courage from their anger to reverse their low aspirations.

You should not necessarily aim low; you usually get less than you aim for. Balance the prize of high aspirations with the price of unfulfilled ambition.

### ASSISTED NEGOTIATION

Getting a neutral third party to assist the parties in reaching a settlement. The assistance may take one of several forms, including mediation, facilitation, or consensus building.

### ASSUMPTIONS

In business, and in affairs of the heart, assumptions are inevitable.

- Check out your assumptions before acting on them.

- Ask QUESTIONS.
- Listen to the answers for what they tell you about your assumptions.

### ASSUMPTIVE CLOSE

A seller's close ploy. The seller asks a question that assumes the prospective buyer has decided to purchase. If the buyer answers the question, he or she commits to buy.

- Will you collect, or shall we deliver?
- Is it cash or charge?
- Do you want them in batches of 50 or 100?

If you are buying, seek additional movement from the seller before you give a BUYING SIGNAL. To block the assumptive close, tell the seller: "I am not in a position to answer these questions until I have decided whether to do business with you. First you must tell me what you propose with respect to . . . ."

### AUCTION

System of selling that puts maximum pressure on buyers.

- In a regular auction buyers call out their bids in an ascending order. The last bidder wins.
- In a DUTCH AUCTION the first bidder wins. The auctioneer calls prices in a descending order.
- In a "Vickery sealed-bid auction" the highest bidder wins at the second-highest bidder's PRICE.

### AUTHORITY

Negotiators without authority leave you vulnerable if the higher authority seeks additional concessions from you in exchange for an **AGREEMENT**. Avoid this by doing one of the following:

- Ask the negotiators whether they have the full authority to settle. Do not necessarily believe the answer you get.

- Hold back something in the proposal for that final traded **CONCESSION** to obtain agreement.

When asked if you have authority when you have not, say yes. Take an **ADJOURNMENT** to "consider the proposal" but use the opportunity to refer it to the decision makers. Claim on your return to the meeting that the required changes resulted from your own consideration of the total package. To assess authority level, ask the following questions:

❏ What are your procedures for making decisions of this nature?

❏ Who in your company participates in these decisions?

❏ How long do decisions of this nature normally take?

### Avoidance-avoidance model

An insight from the field of psychology applied to negotiation.

In brief, people faced with two relatively unattractive choices try to avoid both. The closer they are to an unattractive choice, the more they try to avoid making it. For example, a company's choices are to

- settle on the union's terms;

- stick to its current position and thus risk the costs of a **STRIKE**.

A company wishing to avoid both choices seeks a compromise: a wage increase smaller than the one the union demands, but larger than its own opening **OFFER**.

The union's debate **STRATEGY** aims to

- increase the company's inclination to avoid a strike;
- reduce the company's tendency to avoid meeting the union's current demand.

The union asserts that the costs of a strike are higher than the company's own estimates (see **SECONDARY BOYCOTT**), or that the company's competitors are raising their wages, thus reducing the **RISK** of a competitive disadvantage if it meets the union's claim.

The company's debate strategy aims to

- increase the union's inclination to avoid a **DEADLOCK**;
- decrease the union's tendency to avoid accepting the company's last offer.

## Bagatelle

A presentational ploy to overcome resistance to major changes perceived to be too expensive, onerous, or unacceptable to the other party.

The bagatelle is used by sellers of anything relatively expensive. To protect yourself from the bagatelle, always gross up to the full cost (**PRICE** per slice times the number of slices). To use the bagatelle, break down the total cost of your product into small slices. For instance, sell paper by the sheet, hospital insurance by the daily charge, cable TV by the cost per hour, telephone calls in three-minute units (call Timbuktu for only $3.52).

Time-share companies use a brilliant bagatelle: "A week in Acapulco forever, for the cost of a week in Acapulco."

## Balloon

When the entire loan, plus the accumulated interest, is paid off in one "balloon" payment on a specified date instead of in regular installments.

Lend on balloon terms if you want a large lump sum (the loan plus interest) at some date in the future. You are vulnerable if the borrower does not make provision to repay by the due date and its assets do not cover the loan plus accumulated interest.

Borrow on balloon terms if you expect a large sum (for example, inheritance, sale of an asset) by the due date. If you fail to make provisions for repayment, you put your assets at **RISK**.

If you lend on balloon terms, observe the following:

- Require the borrower to pledge an asset against the loan and the accumulated interest.
- Insist on a standard security over the asset.
- Lend only what you can wait a long time for.
- Inspect the pledged asset regularly.

### BANK

A bank lends money that does not belong to it. If banks do not lend, they go bust. They also go bust if they lend any amount of money at a loss to parties who cannot pay back what they borrow.

Negotiating a loan to finance your lifestyle can be disastrous. You will end up broke, as interest payments gobble up your income (if you have any).

### BARGAINING

Getting something you value highly for something you value less. Bargaining is based on exchanging something for something.

When you buy food in exchange for cash, you value the food more than you do the cash; otherwise you would stay hungry. The seller values the cash more than the food; otherwise it would keep the food. At the moment of the TRADE you each get a bargain.

To bargain, discover what you have that the other party values highly and what they have that you want.

### BARGAINING CONTINUUM

Illustrates the relationship between the offers of two negotiators, the distance between our entry point and theirs. The first OFFER we make is not the final offer we might make.

- We open with our entry point; where we are prepared to move to is our exit point. The distance between them is our negotiable range.
- If our exit points overlap, we could settle anywhere in the overlap. This is the settlement area.
- If our exit points do not meet or overlap we are unlikely to settle.

**Bargaining Continuum**

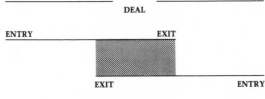

### BARGAINING LANGUAGE

Some forms of language help negotiators, others do not. The following language does not help.

**Q:** I'll increase my **OFFER** by ten. How about that?

**A:** Okay, we'll throw in two extra terminals.

**Q:** If I improve the payback period, will that do?

**A:** We'll cover the insurance costs, okay?

These are unconditional offers. They do not require anything in exchange. An unconditional offer is a movement toward giving in. If the other party is moving at "no cost to you," try asking for more.

Use **CONDITIONAL LANGUAGE**.

- If you pay in 21 days, I'll increase the offer to ten.

- If you buy the standard software, I'll include an extra terminal.
- If you sign the order now, I'll improve the payback period.
- If you pay for full security cover, I'll reduce the insurance charge.

### BARTER

Exchange of goods and services without using cash. Sometimes prevalent in times of war, revolution, hyperinflation, and other disasters. Parties with something to TRADE can try bartering to get what they want. Children barter toys because they have no cash. In the underground economy people trade labor for food, surplus food for timber, surplus household fixtures for whatever they can get for them.

Barter is less efficient than cash, if cash is available, and requires haggling skills.

Remember: it is not what something is worth to you that counts, but what it is worth to the person who wants it.

### BATNA

See BEST ALTERNATIVE TO A NEGOTIATED AGREEMENT

### BEST ALTERNATIVE TO A NEGOTIATED AGREEMENT

Commonly referred to by its acronym, BATNA.

How does the proposal match your realistic alternatives? The more attractive your alternatives to the proposed AGREEMENT, the more POWER you have. The fewer your alternatives and the less attractive they are compared with the results of negotiation, the less power you have.

The following will help develop your **BATNA**.

☐ List anything you could conceivably do if you fail to reach an acceptable agreement.

☐ Convert the most promising alternatives into practical options.

☐ Select your single best **OPTION**. This is your **BATNA**.

☐ Judge all proposals against this **BATNA**.

☐ If the **OFFER** is better than your **BATNA**, consider accepting the offer.

☐ If the offer is worse than your **BATNA**, negotiate for improvement.

☐ If the offer does not improve, exercise your **BATNA**.

## BID

Puts maximum pressure on a supplier.

Suppliers bid on a **ONE-OFFER-ONLY** basis, quoting their "best **PRICE**" for the specified work. Bids are expected to contain a minimum of **PADDING**, provided buyers enforce a one-offer-only procedure and there is no collusion among the bidders.

Allowing bidders to negotiate their bids induces them to pad their first bid, until they see what the competition is quoting. If further discussion is allowed, this weakens the price-squeeze effects on the seller.

## BID LAST

A ploy to maximize your minimal chances of doing better in a competitive bid situation.

If asked to bid competitively for business, and you eagerly send in your bid early, the buyer can use your bid to encourage others to improve on it. Hence, bid last. Hand it over by reliable messenger at the very last possible moment.

If the bidding develops into an AUCTION, proceed as follows.

- Tell them to contact you last and ask for details of the lowest bid.
- Blow the best bid out of the water, or withdraw.
- Never bid more than once in a bid auction: bid last or not at all.

### BID/NO BID

Bidding costs can be high. These costs are recouped if the bid is successful.

If you do not bid, you do not win business. If you bid unsuccessfully, you add to costs. Balancing winning bids with losing bids may not be enough. You must increase the bid-win rate.

If, however, you are overloaded with work, the last thing you need is more work. Bid high, and hope they say "no thanks."

Winning unprofitable bids is not good for business. Hence:

❐ What happens if you do not bid?
❐ What happens if you bid but lose?
❐ What happens if you bid and win?
❐ Is there any VULNERABILITY in the contract terms?
❐ Who are the competitors for the contract?
❐ What can you offer that is as good, different from, or better than the competition?
❐ Where are you vulnerable to competitive pressure?
❐ How can you influence the client to prefer your bid?

❏ Can you emphasize the relationship between in-service costs and initial PRICE?

❏ Can you repackage finance and credit?

❏ Can you highlight the cost of add-ons of spurious specifications ("gold plating")?

❏ Can you offer better after-sales service?

❏ Can you demonstrate high-profile quality assurance systems?

If the answers are positive, deploy resources for the bids. If they are marginal, compare your bids with immediate alternative bids. If they are negative, or insufficiently positive, do not bid.

### BLACKMAIL

Influencing another's behavior by threats to expose something, or to damage something or someone they value. The blackmailer's STRATEGY is to threaten harm unless you comply with his or her demands.

As a TARGET, you can comply with or resist the blackmailer's demands. As a blackmailer, you can reprieve or punish the target.

There are costs in complying:

• Paying money

• Changing a policy

• Releasing the blackmailer's cronies

• Refraining from doing something you would prefer to do

The blackmailer may punish you out of vindictiveness (or to destroy evidence or a witness) or reprieve you if you comply.

If you resist, the costs of the blackmailer implementing his or her THREAT and carrying out the punishment could involve killing a hostage, destroying property, making public something damaging about you, causing havoc, and so on.

You can, however, also benefit from each choice.

- By complying, you avoid the threat of punishment (NET of the consequences to your wealth, policy preferences, respect for law and order, and so on).
- By resisting, you avoid the costs of complying, and may avoid punishment (if the blackmailer is bluffing or is stymied by your resistance).

The outcome depends on the balance of probabilities of the alternative events occurring. The blackmailer aims to convince you that threats will be carried out if you do not comply. If you greatly value the threatened object (the victim, the business, peace, your reputation) and believe that the threat is credible, you are persuaded to comply.

The blackmailer's tactics include enhancing the credibility of the threat (visibly preparing for war or for a STRIKE, demonstrating a capacity for punitive actions). Credibility is also enhanced if there is an inevitability about the threat being imposed. For example, a third party inflicts the punishment automatically if the deadline is not met; or there is a record of imposing punishment in similar circumstances.

Your tactics are limited if the blackmailer's threat is unexpected (a kidnapping, a hijack) and you have little experience dealing with the problem. They include the following:

- Reducing the value to the blackmailer or inflicting punishment by encouraging belief in a positive payoff for a reprieve

- Convincing the blackmailer that you are ready to comply in order to delay punishment
- Stalling while defenses are marshaled against the costs of punishment (prepare for war, stockpile for a strike, arrange alternative supplies, send the police to hunt the kidnapper, make public the incidents the blackmailer is threatening to disclose, and so on).

Under the stress of maintaining vigilance for "tricks," or merely from reviewing the uncertain payoffs of the exercise, blackmailers sometimes reduce their demands to encourage compliance. Experience shows that this encourages resistance because it increases the net benefits to you of noncompliance.

Your willingness to resist depends on the relative payoffs for compliance ($C$) and resistance ($R$). The relative balance between the payoffs (net benefits) decides the appropriate action.

- If $R > C$, you should resist.
- If $C > R$, you should comply.
- If the RISK of punishment is minimal, you should aim for a reprieve.

The blackmailer has a better chance of succeeding if the cost of compliance to you is not unreasonable and the compliance demand is realistic. Unrealistic compliance demands raise the net benefit of resistance.

### BLAME CYCLE

Negotiators get bogged down in blame cycles because identifying the guilty is easier than addressing the problem. Each side raises issues of less and less relevance to the immediate problem. The result is a destructive ARGUMENT. Blame cycles are easy to slide into, time-wasting, difficult to stop, and destructive of a relationship. There are three things to tell anyone with a complaint.

- I am going to apologize on behalf of my people for the stress we have caused you.
- I am going to listen to what you have to say.
- With your help, I am going to put it right.

The complainer usually cools down and becomes conciliatory.

### BLOCKING OFFER

A disreputable ploy. A negotiator appears on the scene offering much better terms than the one on offer. You stop a negotiation with the first party and switch to the newcomer. Once the old negotiation is dead, the new negotiator becomes difficult. There are problems, "unforeseen difficulties," and newly significant small print in the PROPOSAL. You can either settle on the now-much-reduced "better" terms or drop out of the negotiation.

If you try to settle and find the new negotiator drops out, you will know it was only a blocking offer. He or she never intended to do a deal on any terms.

*Counter:* As a condition for dropping the first negotiation, require the new negotiator to purchase an OPTION for a sum at least equivalent to the margin between her bid and the one you have from the first negotiator.

❐ If she settles on the agreed terms, her money is set against the PRICE; if she does not, you keep her money.

❐ Prevarication suggests she is making a blocking offer.

❐ Study her offer very carefully in search of any LIFE-BOAT CLAUSE.

❑ If there is anything in the offer giving her discretion, insist on its removal or amendment.

### BLUFF

Much loved by scriptwriters who have a passing acquaintance with the works of Machiavelli, it is almost always counterproductive. Bluffing is exhilarating from the security of your armchair, but it is cold sweat in the real world.

Avoiding bluffing does not mean you disclose your vulnerabilities. A called bluff is a credibility killer. Your prospects are dead from then on.

### BOBBIN' AND WEAVIN'

A ploy to dodge a powerful assault on your weak flanks.

All positions have weaknesses. Other negotiators search for them. Damage avoidance is called for.

❑ **Parry the attack.** "I could take up that point right now, but I prefer to do so when we have all the facts on the table."

❑ **Acknowledge the problems, but deny their importance.** "Yes, you are right, we did miss that delivery, but against the entirety of our dealings, a missed delivery is hardly the decisive criterion of our competence."

❑ **Refer to TIME constraints.** "I wish we had time to go into all the details and the special circumstances of that case, but if we did, we would be here for hours."

❑ **Refer to NEED TO KNOW status.** "To answer that point properly, I would need to disclose to you highly confidential details, so please do not pursue those matters further without the highest clearance from the boss."

### BOULWARISM

A version of **ONE-OFFER-ONLY** applied to labor contracts.
Named after Lemuel Boulware, vice president of General Electric, who introduced a negotiating stance that
left no room for traditional methods of negotiation.

Boulwarism requires three things:

1. A survey of employee opinion, **ASPIRATIONS**, and attitudes

2. Consideration of what the company wants to do in terms of wages and other conditions of employment

3. Presentation of a total package to the employees that is nonnegotiable

Boulwarism is a major bogey in union mythology.
Because it denies a formal bargaining role to the union,
it produces considerable hostility, especially when introduced suddenly.

Boulwarism is likely to succeed where certain conditions exist:

• Union leadership is discredited.

• Employees are recovering from a prolonged **STRIKE**.

• The market has visibly turned against the products.

• Survival of the company is the primary concern of a majority of the employees.

• Management intelligence has correctly estimated where the shop floor is willing to settle.

Boulwarism is not recommended for the faint of heart
or managements that have not done their homework.

### BRAINSTORMING

Putting options out on the table for discussion in an
uncommitted manner. Frees the brain to conceive of

new options that may break an impasse or consider win-win solutions that have not been thought of previously. Tied to **CREATING NOT CLAIMING**. People often introduce these ideas with "What if . . . ?" (see **WHAT IF?**).

### BRIBERY

Bribery is a crime. It is immoral. It is unethical. It is unfair. It is practiced. Bribery is corruption. It taints all who touch it. But in many parts of the world it is the way business is done. To cynics the boundary between bribery and paying for a service, or permission to do something, is blurred. You know you have crossed the boundary when you are caught.

Do not assume that everybody is on the take: any country's prisons are worse than its hotels.

Greedy people get sticky fingers. A **GO-BETWEEN** will bribe others out of what he or she gets from you. Occasionally, a very important greedy person gets between you and your deal; it costs you a small fortune to get past him. Either pay up or shut up, or shop him and run.

### BRINKMANSHIP

A high-risk enforcement ploy. John Foster Dulles, secretary of state during the 1950s, exemplified diplomacy by brinkmanship. Here is a taste of his philosophy:

*You have to take chances for peace. Just as you must take chances in war. Some say we were brought to the verge of war. Of course we were brought to the verge of war. The ability to get to the verge without gettting into war is the necessary art.*

### BROOKLYN OPTICIAN

A version of the ADD-ON ploy. The seller adds on costs until the buyer flinches. Supposedly worked to effect by a legendary optician in Brooklyn, New York.

The lenses are $90 . . . each. . . . the frames are $40 . . . for the basic shape, like your grandmother wore . . . and $89 for a designer pair . . . plus $30 for fitting . . . in the shop . . . and $50 for a home visit . . . within four blocks. . . . Beyond that it's $5 a block extra. . . . You can have them in five days for $10 . . . a day. Regular brushed steel is $20 . . . a part, and it's $45 if you want gold . . . leaf . . . and 18-carat gold is $30 . . . a lens frame . . . plus state taxes. . . .

Each pause gives the buyer an opportunity to call a halt; no response tells the seller to keep piling on the add-ons.

You can apply the ploy if you know your variables.

* My normal charge is $350 . . . weekends extra.
* That will be $90 . . . plus $30 for delivery . . . tomorrow . . . $45 today.
* The documentation charge is $120 . . . per head.

*Counter:* Flinch and cut in at the first pause.

### BUYING SIGNAL

See one, stop your OFFER. Send one, and the offers stop.

Why? Because buying signals show a willingness to settle on the terms of the current offer, so why offer more?

Examples of buying signals include the following:

* Assumptive ownership ("I'll make this room my study.")

- Issuing instructions for delivery
- Disappointment at lead times for possession
- Concentrated attention to buying details
- Asking QUESTIONS that relate the product or service directly to usage
- Looking intently at the product
- Asking what the spouse/partner thinks
- Showing good humor with the partner (the euphoria of the purchase)
- Positive responses to an ASSUMPTIVE CLOSE

### CAPITULATION

The ultimate CONCESSION.

### CAR-BUYING PSYCHOLOGY

Professional car dealers have at least one advantage over you: they practice their negotiating techniques several times a day, while you try it perhaps once every few years.

When you are buying a volume car, the seller tries to convince you that you can afford it; when you are buying a prestige car (Rolls-Royce, Mercedes, Jaguar), you try to persuade the seller that you can afford it. Either way, the seller has got you.

### CASH

Instant, perfect liquidity. Also easy to lose through theft, accident, and impulse.

Insist on cash in the following situations:

☐ Sooner rather than later
☐ When dealing with unreliable, untrustworthy, or otherwise suspect people
☐ When your banker has closed your account
☐ When your creditors have charge of your assets
☐ When you are unlikely to spend it
☐ When the transaction is dodgy
☐ When it is a NO-COME-BACK deal

Refrain from accepting cash in these situations:

☐ When you are paid in dark alleys
☐ When you can wait for your money

☐ When you have a long journey to make

☐ When you are an impulsive spender

Pay cash in the following situations:

☐ When you do not need a written record

☐ When it helps reduce the PRICE

☐ When you have too much cash on your person

☐ When it gets you additional concessions

Do not pay cash in these situations:

☐ When you need a written record

☐ When you suspect the money is forged

☐ When you might need to cancel the check before it is presented

☐ When you are not sure to whom you are paying it

☐ When there is a delay between payment and the service

### CASH ON DELIVERY (COD)

The purchaser pays cash on delivery of the goods. No credit is allowed. The cash is collected by the deliverer of the goods (before they are handed over), who deducts expenses and passes on the net amount to the supplier. Alternatively, the deliverer pays the net amount to the supplier before delivery and collects the gross amount on delivery.

### CAUCUS

Private time for one side to a negotiation to deliberate alone. Time to think about a new PROPOSAL from the other side. Time to get your act together. Sometimes people ask for time out simply because things are becoming too tense. In negotiations, it is best if each party has its own "space" to which it can go whenever necessary.

## CEILING AND FLOOR

A metaphor for the maximum and minimum requirements for a solution. If one person's floor is the same as another's ceiling, you have an agreement. Mediators try to discover whether there is a gap between one party's floor and the other's ceiling or if there is an overlap. This will determine how easy or difficult it will be to reach an agreement. Ceilings and floors may change throughout a negotiation, and a stated ceiling and floor may not be the real ones. In fact, many agreements are ultimately reached because the parties to them have modified their original ideas of their maximum and minimum.

## CHILDREN

The world's best negotiators. Children
- know how to get what they want;
- are utterly ruthless at having their needs met;
- have no sense of responsibility;
- have no sense of shame or feelings of remorse or notion of guilt;
- have no milk of human kindness;
- have no long-term plans.
  Parents
- give in to their children;
- give in to each other;
- are responsible;

- are easily shamed and in constant states of remorse;
- feel guilty (therefore they are guilty);
- are a font of human kindness (and a bottomless pit for goodies);
- have long-term hopes (pensions, career, retirement, peace, "the best is yet to come").

Result: children win hands down.

They open negotiations on the balance between cabbage and ice cream with a firm refusal to eat any cabbage at all. We invariably start off by threatening "no cabbage, no ice cream." Our futile offers move through "some cabbage, then ice cream," to "just look at the cabbage for a second, and you can have the ice cream." Finally, we give in and pass the ice cream.

The children's strengths are their determination to meet high ASPIRATIONS, to use emotional BLACKMAIL, and to live for their immediate gratification.

But parents have the last laugh because children grow up and acquire a taste for things that can only be acquired through negotiation. (What is courtship but an early attempt at negotiation?) In short, they become conditioned like the rest of us. We win.

### CIRCUMSTANCES

"Broken noses alter faces, circumstances alter cases" is the negotiator's litany when faced with an ambiguous case. The law tries to be tidy. Human relationships create new cases in new circumstances for which the drafters of the rules never planned.

Negotiators establish that the circumstances are unique and that the ordinary rules do not apply. Whether you agree depends on their plausibility, the genuineness of the different circumstances, and the relative inevitability of the precedent being set.

### COALITION

An alliance of parties with a common interest. Negotiations are often conducted between coalitions. This means you must first negotiate within your coalition. Its particular INTERESTS may not correspond completely with yours.

Here are some basic rules.

◻ If you cannot convince your partners of the stance you intend to take, review your chances of convincing others.

◻ Make a COMMAND DECISION if your preparation time is taken up with total disagreement between you and your partners.

◻ Avoid negotiating with more than one STRATEGY, with multiple views on tradable concessions, or with "leaders" who have differing views about negotiable ranges.

Disarray in the other coalition is usually a result of a dispute about negotiating objectives, one lot preferring an accommodation with your view (the moderates), the other demanding a tougher line (the militants).

Take advantage of these divisions to achieve your objectives by assisting the moderate position to prevail, not by crushing the entire coalition.

◻ Support the ideas, not the personalities, of the moderates closest to your position.

◻ If the moderates are the majority of the coalition, propose accommodating moves to isolate the militants.

◻ If the moderates are in a minority, demonstrate that

the payoff for being militant is less than the payoff for being moderate.

Do *not* take advantage by doing any of the following:

❑ Pointedly preferring the moderates

❑ Mocking the other coalition's disarray

❑ Personalizing the coalition's differences

❑ Toughening your demands to the extent that you reunite the coalition

❑ Rewarding or encouraging militancy

Caution: Be aware that the militant-moderate "disarray" may be a GOOD COP/BAD COP ploy.

## COD

See CASH ON DELIVERY

### COERCION

Facing a conflict of INTERESTS, you can coerce your opponent into capitulation.

Coercion can be a two-way process: each side attempts to coerce the other with threats or with violent or expensive actions. You risk having to implement your threats and suffer the consequences. Law courts, strikes, and wars are expensive.

Remember:

• Negotiation is rational if there are high risks of damaging hostilities.

• Coercion is appropriate if there are serious risks of conceding "too much."

Coercion is a commitment ploy to do something unpleasant unless your opponents comply. If they comply, you win, they lose (the Cuban missile crisis). They can also countercommit, forcing you to do what you threatened. Fear of the high costs of failure drives you both into negotiating stances.

To back off from coercion:

❏ Reduce the imminence of your threats.

❏ Extend to vague deadlines.

❏ Minimize outright provocation.

Peace can still fall apart with one miscalculated move.

### COLLATERAL

Almost anything that the lender will accept as cover for the RISK of lending you money is collateral. For example, the lender holds one part and you keep the other such as high-value notes, or bearer bonds.

Borrowers arrange a loan against an item of greater value than the loan. If you default on the loan, the lender makes a profit by selling the collateral. To serve as collateral the item must be of sufficient value

• to encourage your repayment of the loan;

• to cover the lender's loss if you do not.

Your risks in accepting items as collateral include the possibility that the borrower does not own them.

### COLLECTIVE BARGAINING

Jointly determined rules for the use of labor in employment.

The rules are negotiated by unions either directly with an employer or with an AGENT of the employer and cover the following areas:

- Remuneration
- Hours of work
- Types of work
- Performance standards
- Holidays and other entitlements
- Flexibility
- Restrictions
- Layoffs
- Standards
- Work rates
- Overtime
- Retirement provisions
- Promotion
- Responsibilties and obligations of the bargaining agents
- Relationships between the bargaining agents
- Definitions of reasonable conduct
- Disciplinary procedures
- Procedures for resolving disputes

There are efficiency benefits to management in having collective agreements with bargaining agents representing employees because individual negotiations could produce different rules for each employee. There are costs too. The bargaining agent

- interferes with managerial independence;
- urges employees to show loyalty to, and accept discipline from, the union;
- can initiate disruption in the company;
- can introduce an internal division that cuts across

or threatens a company culture based on excellence, pride, self-respect, and mutual goal seeking.

Should you join a union?

❏ No, if the relative gains from bargaining for yourself exceed those of hiring someone else to do it for you.

❏ Yes, if the agent has the superior detailed expertise (that is, deals with similar issues every day).

❏ No, if the union concentrates its effort on modest gains for the collective rather than larger gains for the individual.

### COMMAND DECISION

When a negotiating team cannot agree on a tactic or style appropriate to the circumstances, or cannot agree on the contents of an OFFER, the most senior negotiator can make a command decision by virtue of rank alone. The decision carries its own authority and the team falls into line. Command decisions are not necessarily correct decisions, but the wrong decision may be better than no decision. The person making a command decision must take full responsibility; reckless use of a commander's privileges carries penalties.

### COMMISSION

Payment for services rendered, for exceeding sales targets, for introducing clients, and so on (see BRIBERY).

Because the gross value of an income stream is always larger than the net value,

• propose that your commission is a percentage of gross rather than net value;

• offer a commission as a percentage of net rather than gross value.

Gross values keep the negotiator honest. Net value is open to ambiguity:

- Net of what?

- Who decides the deductibles?

Avoid statements offering you percentages of "earnings from the contract that directly arise from your efforts."

- "Earnings" after their accountants have had a go will not amount to much.

- "Directly arises" confines you to quibbles about how much you did and how much they had to do after you set it up.

### COMMITMENT PLOY

Methods to make a THREAT credible. For example, unless other parties comply with your demands, you can bind yourself to an irrevocable course of action that would do immense damage to them, irrespective of what damage it does to you. The more certain your commitment (you die too), the more credible your threat and the more likely they will comply.

To apply commitment:

❑ Make it known.

❑ Show that you mean what you say.

Dire warnings of the consequences of your commitment (plant closures, job losses, long strikes, war, and so on) reinforce the impact of your commitment. ("This negotiator is irrational, I had better be more careful.")

Undermine the commitment of others by using so-called salami ploys. A specific threat to boycott, STRIKE, launch a thermonuclear war, unless you comply is vulnerable to minute challenges:

- They demand a meeting by April 10; you offer one on April 11.
- They demand progress to reform in six months; you schedule talks about it for eight months (then query the details of arrangements).
- They demand no more than 10% penetration of their markets by your EXPORTS; you send 10.43%.

Salami counters undermine commitment because the threat is disproportionate to the challenge. By carefully extending the challenge in size and number, you widen the credibility gap between their commitment and their behavior.

### COMMUNICATION

Messages are misunderstood, misinterpreted, and mislaid.

- The message sent is not always the one received.
- The receivers may entirely miss the significance of your message.
- They need not believe what you are saying.
- They could doubt the source of the message.
- Your message does not make sense to them.

Threats, promises, and commitments have little effect if they cannot be communicated.

We communicate by what we say, how we say it, and our body language. The last accounts for a greater proportion of the message received than the other two combined. If our gestures say something different from our speech, and this is perceived by the receiver, we have a credibility problem.

A written communication can be reread many times.

- It has the benefit of permanence.

- It has the drawback of inflexibility.
- It does not score highly on subtlety and nuance.

This is why others react negatively to what they perceive to be your written insults, callousness, abruptness, and threats, particularly in the difficult phase of a negotiation where the parties are debating the issues closely.

Use the telephone to bolster your firmness. It is easier to say no on the telephone than to say it face-to-face. Use the fax to make inquiries, quote first offers, and confirm agreement (it is not as good for negotiating complex proposals).

### COMPETITIVE STYLE

Competitive negotiators try to win at any cost, which is why they lose. The competitive style is abrasive. The other negotiator is an enemy, not an ally. Anything he or she gets is at your expense. It is total war and ZERO SUM.

### CONCESSION

Never concede anything: TRADE.

### CONCESSION DILEMMA

Consider the gap between the current offers of two negotiators. You are constrained by a desire not to concede anything. You are in conflict with the other negotiator as to the extent of your mutual concessions. You aim to do better than CAPITULATION. Questions with uncertain answers include the following:

- How far must you move?
- How far will he or she move?
- Is a refusal a genuine inability to agree to your present terms or is the other party testing your resolve?

From the other party's point of view:

- Your last OFFER could have been your final offer, but he or she has no way of knowing what is in your mind.

- Should he or she meet your increasing resistance to moving further by edging toward a settlement, or by pressing for more movement?

- Is your last offer a prelude to increased resistance, or to your capitulation?

### CONCESSION RATE

Negotiators who move quickly at first and then stop are likely to frustrate other negotiators because

- the early movement created EXPECTATIONS;
- the later nonmovement frustrated them.

Negotiators who move slowly at first and then quickly are likely to harden the stance of other negotiators because the quicker movement signals that a hard line produces results.

Negotiators who sometimes move quickly and sometimes move slowly provoke pressure from other negotiators, who do not know how else to get movement.

Negotiators who move slowly do better because their consistency is predictable; if they move only in response to a TRADE, they also signal how to get movement.

### CONCESSION SIGNAL

Negotiators who have a reputation for hardly moving once they make their proposals induce other negotiators to attempt to delay them from making their proposals until some influence has been exerted.

Negotiators who move in diminishing steps, starting with relatively large concessions and ending with smaller and smaller concessions, signal that an exit PRICE is being approached.

Negotiators who move unpredictably, sometimes offering a large concession followed by a small one and sometimes the reverse, induce other negotiators to look for large concessions each time and to be disappointed if they are not forthcoming.

### CONCILIATION

Alternative form of dispute resolution (see MEDIATION) to reconcile the parties in dispute, not to judge between them. Useful in fractious cases where the normal relationship between the parties has broken down.

### CONDITIONAL LANGUAGE

States the negotiator's terms for settling an issue. "Give me some of what I want, and I will give you some of what you want."

Effective negotiators use conditional language when making an OFFER.

- On condition that . . .
- Provided that . . .
- If you will do such and such, then I will agree to do so and so.

Conditional language educates the other negotiators in how the issue can be settled.

### CONFLICT

A reason for negotiating.

We cannot negotiate a variance in views, beliefs, attitudes, INTERESTS, actions, desires, needs, ASPIRATIONS, intentions, hopes, dispositions, EXPECTATIONS, principles, and values, but we can negotiate the practical applications of them and the competition for a scarce resource, be it tangible or intangible.

Irreconcilable conflicts are resolved by "live and let live" or the outright triumph of one side. The decision is "peace or war."

Reconcilable conflicts are resolved by PERSUASION, PROBLEM SOLVING, MEDIATION, ARBITRATION, or negotiation. The decision is "debate or TRADE."

### CONFLICT OF INTERESTS AND RIGHTS

When parties have differing notions about their relationship or the terms of doing business together, they have a conflict of INTERESTS. When parties dispute the application of an agreed-on PROCEDURE, as in a disciplinary case, they have a conflict of rights.

"Interests" and "rights" are common terminologies in COLLECTIVE BARGAINING to distinguish how the conflict is to be resolved — within the terms of existing procedures (conflict of rights), including reinterpretation of clauses (through a judicial or quasi-judicial process), or through fresh negotiations to create a new AGREEMENT (conflict of interests).

### CONSENSUS

Building broad agreement among multiple parties for a solution. Often part of negotiation where the government is a party. Usually reached by discussion and general agreement ("If I hear no disagreement, then we can assume that . . . .") rather than by voting.

### CONSTANT SUM

Jargon from GAME THEORY. Where the sum of the payoffs to the negotiator remains the same across all possible solutions to the dispute. (See ZERO SUM)

### Consulting fee

Why do some consultants make more money than others? Because many consultants do not appreciate why they are being consulted.

Consultants are hired for their expertise, yet most of them sell their *time* instead of their expertise. Time costs less than expertise. A consultant's expertise is valuable because it saves clients the time and expense of acquiring it themselves.

Many experts think in terms of what it legitimately costs them to provide the advice. The formula is this: divide annual gross salary costs by the number of available working days, add a margin for administrative costs and a margin for profit, and charge out services at a daily rate.

The alternative method is to charge a percentage of the gross value of your advice to the client.

### Contingency pricing

A method of pricing an uncertain value.

Valuations of the future worth of a business are as variable as the parties' INTERESTS. Buyers understate future worth, sellers exaggerate it. To set the PRICE for the business, offer a basic price that is less than the seller is demanding, plus an amount contingent on whether the future conforms to the seller's opinion or to the buyer's.

- Buyer's downside. The future is a result of the buyer's beneficial contribution, and not just the intrinsic worth of future business.
- Seller's downside. The buyer controls the business and can influence its future performances to understate its true worth.

## CONTRACT LAW

A highly technical subject monopolized by lawyers. The advice offered here is a commonsense summary of the main principles, which inevitably apply differently in each country.

A contract determines the terms under which a business or personal relationship is conducted. It is enforceable at law (though enforceability varies in different countries).

Usually an OFFER to contract is valid if the parties communicate their intentions to be under contract to one another and if the bargain is specified (that is, if there is a consideration). If an offer is unconditionally accepted, there is an enforceable contract (providing the subject of the contract is not illegal). An offer lapses if acceptance is unduly delayed and can be withdrawn on communicating this to the other party before it accepts.

An offer to contract is accepted if the acceptance is unconditional, is communicated to the offerer by the named offeree, and does not amend the offered contract.

A contract is valid unless you can prove duress, fraud, illegality, or undue influence.

Contracts consist of six main elements.

1. The identity and location of the contracting parties
2. What they are contracting to do
3. Their rewards for performing the contract
4. The penalties for nonperformance
5. Duration, legal basis, reversion, and revision rules
6. Confirmed signatures of the parties

Contracts can be amended by agreement of both parties. Contracts may be modified based on changed or unforeseen circumstances, or considered void based on impossibility.

### COOPERATIVE STYLE

Negotiators are cooperative antagonists.

Your antagonisms arise from your conflicting or competing goals; your cooperation arises when DEADLOCK leaves you both worse off than compromise.

### COPYRIGHT

Copyright in a book, a play, or any creative script lasts for your lifetime plus 50 years. Your estate earns ROYAL-TIES after your death. After a copyright lapses, anyone can publish your work without paying royalties.

❏ Insist on retaining your copyright.

❏ Do not give it authority to assign your license to third parties.

❏ Insist that if it fails to meet the terms of the contract or goes bankrupt, the license unconditionally reverts to you.

❏ Do not let liquidators of publishers treat your copyright as a forfeited asset.

### CORRUPTION

No way to do business, but in many places the only way to get into, and around, some countries just to look for business, or simply to stay out of trouble. (See BRIBERY)

### COST BREAKDOWN

Worth getting if it identifies the TRADABLES and the PAD-DING. Volunteering one, however, gives the other side ideas.

To get a detailed breakdown, show a written policy from your organization requiring a breakdown before an order is placed.

To resist supplying a breakdown:

- Show a written policy prohibiting your organization, or yourself, from giving one.
- Claim that "proprietary information," and so on, is at stake.
- Refer the buyer to your competitors' prices, and assert that this is the deciding factor, not how you go about your business.

### COUNTERTRADE

A complex form of BARTER that can take several forms.

- **Counterpurchase.** The parties agree to a linked protocol to purchase equivalent amounts of goods from each other, using foreign currency.
- **Buy-back.** The provider buys back the output of a plant it provides to the other country.
- **Bilateral clearing.** The parties export goods, paid for in local currencies, that are credited against an agreed-on total.
- OFFSET. The buyer is compensated for a purchase by the seller agreeing to purchase goods to an agreed-on value from the buyer country.

Traders without hard currency can exchange goods instead. The financing is done locally for each party under its own arrangements. The practice is common where trade finance is weak or the political risks are high.

Some goods offered for countertrade are unconnected to the goods supplied. When the goods have obvious commercial value, ask why they don't sell the goods themselves and pay you from the proceeds. If you do not want to countertrade, say no firmly and repeatedly.

The goods are not always of obvious value. Sellers pad the value of the goods they offer, so challenge whatever PRICE they put on them. It is not the countertrader's price, but the selling price (NET of transport, insurance, RISK, and marketing) of goods in your own or a third country that counts.

If they spring a countertrade deal on you after a money price has been agreed on for some goods you plan to sell to them, they could be bluffing to finesse additional discounts from you; it is only a device to lower your money price.

#### COURTESY

Nobody ever got a worse deal by being courteous.

#### CREATING, NOT CLAIMING

The idea of having all parties try to solve a problem by creating a solution not previously thought of, rather than claiming their piece of the pie. Creating tends to let the size of the pie increase. (See ENLARGING THE PIE)

#### CREDIT

Give it, and pay it when due.

#### CREDIT CONTROL

It is easier to avoid debts than to collect them.
- ❏ Know who owes you money.
- ❏ Require debtors to establish their creditworthiness.

❏ Set predetermined limits on amounts allowed to be outstanding.

❏ State the days allowed to be overdue.

❏ State the time allowed to pay.

❏ Set rates of repayment.

❏ Seek COLLATERAL for the loan.

If you are running into repayment problems, inform your creditors early because they trust debtors who talk to them in advance marginally more than those who are evasive. An unexplained debt excites suspicions and receives most of the energetic attention of credit controllers.

When renegotiating a rescheduling of a debt, you increase your leverage with its size, for a large debt is a shared problem but a small one is yours alone.

### CULTURAL DIFFERENCES

They count. In a "foreign" country, you are the foreigner. It is you who are the odd one out. Everything the natives do is perfectly natural where they live and work. You with your strange ways must adapt to them, not them to you, assuming you want to do business with them.

Take account of the differences, and accommodate to them where possible.

❏ If the Japanese pace of negotiation is slower than yours, then you had better slow down.

❏ If the American pace is faster, you had better speed up.

❏ If Arabs are not disciplined by TIME, then allow for it when negotiating with them.

❒ If Russians are suspicious, do not behave suspiciously.

❒ If the Chinese keep asking the same QUESTIONS and do not appear to take "no" for an answer, answer patiently with variations on "no."

In short, abide by the advice of travelers going to Rome.

## DEADLINES

Can help or hinder, depending on who discloses that they have one.

Deadlines put you under pressure. But this pressure is nothing compared with the pressure you attract if you disclose your deadlines to the other negotiators.

Will they take advantage of your predicament? Yes. It stiffens their resolve not to move toward you; they know that you will soon be leaping toward them. Hence, do not disclose deadlines that the other negotiators have no other means of knowing about.

Deadlines that help you are those that

- force the other negotiators to decide;
- the other negotiators disclose;
- the other negotiators do not control;
- impose costs on the others;
- give you options;
- you control;
- they know you will stick by.

Deadlines that hinder you are those that

- are arbitrary;
- are imposed by your own people;
- the other parties know about;
- are imminent;
- remove your discretion;
- cannot be ignored.

### DEADLOCK

We negotiate because we face the deadlock of disagreement. Unblocking deadlock could be a victory for good sense or bad judgment. It depends on whether and what we TRADE to get an AGREEMENT. Many companies go bust because they negotiate unprofitable agreements, not because they cannot find enough customers.

If the most the buyer offers is less than the least the seller will except, deadlock is inevitable unless one or both change their exit PRICE.

Single-issue BARGAINING is more prone to deadlock: you resist conceding when you get nothing back (ZERO SUM). Widen the issues, increase the AGENDA, be creative with the PACKAGING of the tradable variables.

Deadlocked on price?

❑ Pay in some other way.

❑ Pay less now, more later.

❑ Pay more now, less later.

❑ Pay some in cash, the rest in kind.

❑ Pay in another currency in another country.

❑ Split the invoice across different budgets.

Deadlocked on a single issue?

❑ Compensate by movement on another issue.

❑ Link several issues together.

❑ Set the issue aside while settling the other issues.

Deadlocked on the value of future trade?

❑ Apply CONTINGENCY PRICING: if your estimate materializes, your price applies; if theirs materializes, their price applies.

Deadlocked across the issues?

❏ Amend the specification. (What are marginal changes in performance worth?)

❏ Alter the time structure of events.

❏ Change the responsibilities. (Who delivers? Who inspects? Who insures? Who secures? Who warrants? Who risks? Who owns?)

❏ Change the nature of the business. (Examples: from production to distribution; from homemade to imported; from foreign to local ownership; from ownership to management; from management to ROYALTIES; from royalties to buyout.)

Deadlock ploys play on negotiators' FEAR OF DEADLOCK. If they "fail" to agree, they anticipate pressures from the people behind them. Hence they move rather than lose.

To threaten deadlock:

❏ Talk up the difficulties of reaching an agreement.

❏ Introduce phony deadlines.

❏ Stage phony walkouts.

❏ Exhibit phony temper.

❏ Become unavailable.

❏ Demonstrate pessimism.

❏ Accuse them of not wanting an agreement.

❏ Make "final offers."

*Counter:* show no fear of deadlock.

### DEBT COLLECTING

Not for the squeamish, the gullible, or the saintly. A bad debt is like theft, except you know the name of the thief.

- Some people do not pay and never intended to pay.
- Some people intended to pay but find it convenient not to pay.
- Some people do not pay because they cannot pay.
- Some people pay only if you make them pay.

Letters and phone calls are useful to a point, but hard-nosed debtors develop plausible imaginations.

- The check is in the mail.
- I am in conference with my accountant and will call you back.
- Check with your bank, our check number was . . . dated the . . . of last month.

*Counters:* What leverage do you have? Can you run up debts using their services to the value of the money they owe you? When they try to collect, reveal the net balance and call it quits.

Collecting debts is best done in person. Invariably you can collect something toward payment (do not be snowed with a promise).

No debt is ever a matter of principle. If you find yourself believing that it is, consider: How much can you make while you are tied up with an obsession about principles?

Remember, any payment — including in kind — is better than none.

### Debt swamp

Swamps are not just messy, they can kill you.

A debt swamp has an inevitability about it. The more you struggle, the deeper you sink.

In the debt swamp you borrow money for a purchase (a house, a car, a yacht). These have costs (taxes, repairs, maintenance, and so on) as does the loan (interest and principal). If the costs of the loan total more than your income, you get your feet wet in the swamp.

If you have insufficient income, you can borrow the difference and get more than your feet wet. As the debt swamp rises, your insufficient income is squeezed. In desperation you turn to a lender and borrow to keep the swamp down; but borrowing more puts you deeper into the swamp.

### DECISION ANALYSIS

A negotiator's preparation tool.

To choose a course of action (whether to or not, whether to go in high or low, whether to take what is on or not, and so on), estimate the value of the competing outcomes and the probability of their being realized.

Estimate the probabilities on the basis of experience. In general, choosing an action with a very high value may mean simultaneously reducing the probability of achieving it. Increasing the probability of success by making it more likely to be acceptable means reducing the expected value of the outcome.

Each outcome is given a value ($V$) and a probability ($p$) of its occurring. $V \times p = EV$ gives its expected value.

Set a minimum expected value to assess the probable outcomes against and calculate the expected values of each OPTION.

For example, if the value of the contract is \$200 and your estimate of the probability of being successful is 60%, then the expected value of the outcome is \$200 $\times$

0.6 = $120. But you have negotiating costs too, and the probability of your proposal being unsuccessful is 1 − 0.6 = 0.4.

The expected value to you of being unsuccessful is your negotiating cost (say, $20) times the probability of this event occurring: $20 × 0.4 = $8. Now the expected value of negotiating for the contract is the sum of the expected values of each event: $120 − 8 = $112. If this is higher than your minimum expected value, negotiate for the contract; if lower, do not.

The analysis can be extended to cover more complex decisions, although the principle is the same.

#### DELAYING TACTIC

TIME changes the balance of POWER and we need tactics to avoid a decision.

Take two belligerents considering the future of their war. The fortunes of war wax and wane. Negotiations are unlikely while the sides have different opinions of their fortunes.

Consider a war where each side recognizes that continued conflict is unproductive. Suppose peace negotiations begin. What do the negotiators do if there is an unexpected military reverse for one of the parties? At the very least, the winning side has a strong incentive to slow down the negotiations, for each day's delay strengthens its bargaining power.

Delaying tactics include the following:

- Quibbling about details
- Taking longer adjournments
- Seeking further instructions
- "Diplomatic" illness

- Celebrating national holidays
- Provoking rows
- Feigning insults
- Changing the members of the delegation
- Raising old issues
- Insisting on full translations
- Requesting changes of venue
- Canceling meetings
- Starting late
- Finishing early

Similar tactics can be used in strikes that swing one way and then the other.

### DELIVERY

Charge for it as an ADD-ON; demand it as a DISCOUNT.

### DEVIL'S ADVOCATE

A preparation tool. A negotiator takes the role of expressing positions directly contrary to the ones prepared by the team. This tests your arguments for soundness and consistency.

Thinking through your proposed responses to the arguments advanced by the devil's advocate tests their credibility and exposes deficiencies in the data or PREPARATION, which allows you time to fill in the gaps.

### DICKER

See HAGGLE

### DISAGGREGATING THE PROBLEM

Used in negotiation to focus on a piece of the problem as a way of untying the knot of conflict. Sometimes disaggregation is referred to as "uncoupling" pieces of a problem that have previously been linked. Having both parties begin to elaborate on the elements of the total problem is a way of creating an AGENDA of issues. Then discussing one element can be a way of building trust if progress is made on that issue. Negotiators may move back and forth between easier and harder issues, eventually putting each element together in a package.

## DISCOUNT

A deduction from a PRICE.

Discounts are given for all kinds of reasons. Some are common in particular businesses and have a habit of growing into permanent features of an invoicing system because they set precedents.

Among other reasons, invoices may be discounted to encourage the following:

- Payment on time
- Large-volume orders
- Payment in advance
- Payment of something on an overdue account
- Customer loyalty
- Placement of an order before a set date

After the event, the client expects the discount to continue. Rival suppliers respond to price discounting by offering discounts themselves. The result is a PRICE WAR.

Negotiators should always ask for discounts and should be creative about the reasons they require them. Discounts can be demanded credibly for any of the following:

❐ Early payment
❐ Advance payment
❐ Payment of a deposit
❐ Large volume
❐ Purchase of several items
❐ The right to use your name in supplier advertising
❐ End-of-stock purchase
❐ First-of-stock purchase
❐ Reward for recommending supplier to other customers
❐ Loyalty to supplier over the years
❐ First-time use of supplier
❐ Placing all your business with supplier
❐ Placing some of your business on introductory basis
❐ Seasonal purchases
❐ Delivery at awkward times
❐ Rescheduled deliveries
❐ Instant delivery
❐ Delayed delivery
❐ Collecting from supplier base with own transport
❐ Missed delivery
❐ Incomplete or mistaken order
❐ Any inconvenience caused by supplier

### DISTRIBUTIVE BARGAINING

Examples of distributive bargaining include the following:

- A wage increase that increases employees' incomes and employer's costs

- A price negotiation that benefits the buyer and reduces the income of the seller
- A boundary or territorial negotiation by which one
  country reduces the territory of another

The algebraic sum of the gains and losses produces
ZERO SUM outcomes (see also INTEGRATIVE BARGAIN-
ING).

If we divide a scarce resource between us, what you
gain I lose. Conflict, however, is not unbounded. Neither of us can get our own way entirely (if we could, we
would not bother negotiating).

Do not negotiate when you are

- in a hurry,
- exhausted,
- emotionally involved,
- sexually aroused,
- busy with other tasks,
- late for an appointment,
- bored,
- angry,
- under pressure,
- meant to be elsewhere,
- desperate,
- under the influence of drink or drugs,
- euphoric,
- suspicious,
- jet-lagged,
- hungry, or
- in need of a visit to the rest room.

## DUTCH AUCTION

If you have two or more bids for the same item, instead of selling to the highest or buying from the lowest bidder, contact each bidder separately and offer them an opportunity to improve on their rival's last BID. This term commonly is misused.

Keen buyers rebid just above their rivals, and keen sellers cut their prices to just below those of their rivals, in the hope of winning. Try several rounds of quoting and requoting the last bid to the rivals (and why not, if the bidders want to keep bidding?) until only one bidder survives.

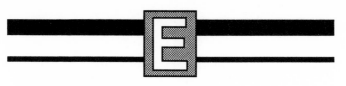

## Either/or Thinking

To be avoided in negotiation. Reflects a win/lose, all-or-nothing approach. Sometimes the best solution will be neither/both and usually it is something entirely new.

## Emotion

Used sparingly, emotion can help a negotiator express commitment. There are emotional traps in

- sending messages;
- signaling EXPECTATIONS;
- underlining a THREAT or PROMISE;
- establishing RAPPORT;
- overcoming obstacles;
- reinforcing TRUST;
- altering PERCEPTION.

CONFLICT generates emotions and can be an obstacle to progress; it can inhibit judgment of self-interest; it can protract a negotiation and provoke DEADLOCK.

To reduce emotional tension, observe the following guidelines:

❑ Refrain from exciting INHIBITIONS.

❑ Never mock the weaknesses or setbacks of the other party.

❑ Demonstrate willingness to understand, if not to agree with, the other party's views and INTERESTS.

❑ Refrain from emotional attacks.

❑ Do not challenge the other party's motives, integrity, or legitimacy.

Faced with an emotional outburst either in attack or defense, remain calm. Emotion subsides more quickly if it is not fed.

It is difficult to eliminate emotions when you have strong feelings for or against the other negotiator for some reason (family, friendship, love, sympathy, likeability, solidarity, suspicion, distrust, previous dirty tricks, duplicity, unfulfilled promises, and such). But deals led by emotions, positive or negative, are worse deals than those that you remain clearheaded about.

### ENLARGING THE PIE

The notion that if you focus on trying to meet your own INTERESTS but are not opposed to meeting the interests of the other party so long as they do not conflict with yours in a fundamental way, then the solution may end up better for both. We think of this as enlarging the pie rather than carving up an existing one. This concept comes from GAME THEORY and the Pareto optimum, in which the purpose of negotiation becomes trying to attain as many wins for each side as possible. Often achieved by repackaging those elements that have been previously disaggregated.

### ESCALATION

A measured pressure ploy, sometimes used unethically. Jumping from peace to all-out war is unusual. First, a little pressure is applied, then some more, and eventually full pressure is imposed.

If DEADLOCK is caused by the other negotiators' unreasonable obstinacy, the escalation might work. Their obstinacy, however, might be caused by your unreasonable (as they perceive them) demands. Your escalating pressure only convinces them that you are being unreasonable. You risk a mixture of indignation and **MARTYR-DOM**, which results in stiffening resistance rather than surrender.

### ESCALATOR SCHEDULE

A formula to increase an agreed-on share in uncertain future income streams. Publishers normally agree to escalate an author's **ROYALTIES** as sales reach specified quantities. Similarly, anyone owning rights to a product should negotiate escalator clauses in licensing agreements.

Tactically, your aim is to increase the royalty or fee and decrease the qualifying amount that triggers off the increased royalty (reverse this if you are acquiring the license).

If negotiating **COMMISSION** terms (or performance-related pay), go for an escalator clause: so much for reaching a performance level and extra for exceeding it. It is better to negotiate this before improving performance (see **HOOKER'S PRINCIPLE**).

### ETHICS

If you want to influence others, do not preach to them about your ethics. There is not a lot to choose from between the unethical and the sanctimonious.

You should take into account the potential costs of unethical conduct, including the attention of the law, public contempt, and damage to your **REPUTATION**.

### EXCHANGE

How decisions are made by negotiation. You exchange things you have for things you want; you exchange your consent for a consideration.

#### EXPECTATIONS

You have them: they help determine your strategies and your objectives. If your expectations are unrealizable, or you come to believe that they are, you adjust them or pursue a hopeless quest (see **POWER**).

#### EXPORT CREDIT

World trade must be financed by credit to the buyer and credit to the seller waiting for payment.

Your options for ensuring payment include the following:

- Cash with order. If you can get it.
- **Documentary credit.** Payment on presentation of shipping documents to buyer's bank (insist that the credit is "irrevocable," and "confirmed" so that you can receive payment at your local bank).
- **Transferable credit.** When you are selling as an **AGENT**, your supplier wants payment when you order the goods for your buyer, but you do not get paid until the goods are shipped to the buyer. The solution is to arrange a documentary credit from your buyer in the normal way, but get its bank to pay your supplier its **PRICE** to you on proof of shipping the goods to you (this money is deducted from the documentary credit held in your name). When you ship the goods on to the buyer, you receive the balance of the credit on presentation of your shipping documents.
- **Back-to-back credit.** Use of the documentary credit in your favor from your buyer as security to establish a credit in your supplier's favor, paid when it ships the goods. Less favorable to you than a transferable credit.

- **Revolving credit.** For regular routine transactions that permit a cycle of credit to operate: as one transaction is paid on presentation of the appropriate documents, another is opened.
- **Acceptance credit.** A bank credits you with an amount that you can draw against, and the bank places your bills in the money market; as the buyer's credits to you become due, they are collected by the bank to cover the acceptance allowed to you on the strength of your transaction with the buyer.

You can use your EXPECTATIONS of getting paid by a buyer (the credit system you negotiate) to raise finance. The credit is an asset, albeit a paper one.

You can sell the credit for a discounted price, the purchaser collecting the difference as its gross profit when the documentary credit is paid. Your obligation to ship the goods remains; indeed, the purchaser of the bill can sue you (recourse) if you do not.

### EXPORTS

Without them we would all be poorer; yet everywhere, otherwise sensible people seek to curb one another's.

Exporting is complicated. Frontiers are jealously guarded. Legal systems differ around the world, and disputes between people in separate territories — with the goods, perhaps, in a third territory or in transit between them — add to the normal complexities (and costs). The number of intermediaries involved in shipping goods imposes heavy demands on comprehensive documentation, title to ownership, transfer of ownership, and timely payment as agreed between seller and buyer.

At a minimum, documentation is required to describe the goods, to value them, and to authenticate the declaration. The shipper has numerous formalities to complete too. These formalities and their associated costs incline the prudent seller toward an ex-factory PRICE for the goods, leaving the hassle of exporting to the buyer.

## FACTORING

Invoices are bought by a factoring agent, that collects payment from the buyers and pockets the difference between what it pays for the invoices and what it collects.

The factoring agent eliminates known bad payers, or potential bad payers, and requires a larger margin on some others. Some agents use the supplier's own letterhead, so buyers are unaware they are dealing with a factor.

The spread between the factoring PRICE and the invoice's face value is negotiable, as is whether the factor has recourse to the seller in the case of a bad debt.

## FAIR

A sense of fairness influences negotiators (see NASH SOLUTION). If you were asked what you regard as a fair distribution of a large sum of money between you and a colleague, and you were given no additional information, it is likely that you would prefer an "equal" distribution.

Fairness as a settlement option is popular with economists because their negotiation models do not incorporate bargaining skills, power perceptions, and EXPECTATIONS. By eliminating these, the settlement must end up at the midpoint because there is no economic reason why it should end up anywhere else.

Fairness, however, is not a principle of nature; it is a construct of the mind. "Fairness" can be an objective standard — even if people interpret it differently — that both parties may agree on and that helps move toward agreement. (See PRINCIPLES 2)

### Fait accompli

A ploy to shift POWER to the doer and raise the stakes if countersanctions are applied.

Armies seize territory and then offer to negotiate; a developer knocks down a unique building and then applies for planning permission; managers introduce new work schedules and then agree to negotiations; buyers send a check for a lesser amount than the disputed invoice; a buyer returns goods outside warranty and refuses to pay; a department occupies disputed office space and offers to talk.

*Counter:* Include in your contract firm rules on what cannot be done without invoking heavy legal penalties.

### Fallback position

If you have not got one, then stand and fight where you are. But it's best to think ahead about a fallback position if the negotiations do not work out as you expected. (See BATNA)

### Fear of deadlock

Common enough in negotiation. The fear inhibits negotiators from standing firm, encourages goodwill concessions, and opens them to exploitation. Deadlock implies failure, and we do not like to fail. Much better for us to overcome the fear — and certainly never disclose it.

### Final offer

If you make one, mean it; otherwise do not make one. Final offers are risky and are foolhardy at the beginning of a negotiation. Final offers that become final offers but one (or two, or three) are disastrous for credibility. A final offer bluff, if called, is embarrassing.

To make final offers, pay attention to your language. If no more movement is possible — you are at your exit point and prefer no deal to one on worse terms — say so. A badly phrased final offer, however, is a provocative ultimatum. Tell them

- you can go "no further";
- you are at the "end of the road";
- that it is "decision time."

None of these statements mentions final offer, but that is how it will be perceived.

Do not ask, "Is that your final offer?" The answer you get will not be the one you want. The other negotiators can hardly say no (the answer you want) without compromising their position; hence they are most likely to say yes, blocking off the negotiation.

### First offer

Never accept a first offer: negotiate.

The first offer is where the other parties open; it is not where they expect to end up. If it is, they are in such a powerful position there is no need to negotiate.

If you accept their first offer, what other offers would you accept?

### Fixed price

Sellers love fixed prices because they preclude **BAR-GAINING**. That is why they write prices on large tickets, print price lists, have standard terms for doing business, and imply that the price on the tag is fixed for good.

And why not? Most people accept fixed prices. Few challenge them, fewer still persist after the first no.

But the price on the tag or on the printed list is the **FIRST OFFER**. Whether it is the **FINAL OFFER** remains to be seen.

More often than not, the aversion to negotiating a better price has nothing to do with the buyer's relative **POWER**. It is part of the business culture you live in. In the United Kingdom 97% of people accept the seller's first offer; in the United States it is down as low as 17% in some commodity groups; in Australia it is about 30%.

In business transactions, however, effective negotiators do not accept the price they are first quoted.

- They **HAGGLE**.
- They try to open up first offers to discussion.
- They see what other offers are lurking in the background. (See **DISCOUNT**)

### FLEXIBILITY

In short supply among average negotiators. Flexibility in approach, not **INTERESTS**, comes from thorough **PREPARATION**. The above-average negotiator is armed with options both as to goals and as to methods of achieving them.

### FORCE MAJEURE

Events outside the control of the contracting parties that prevent a contractual obligation from being met. Revolution, war, seizure of assets, embargoes, economic sanctions, geological and climatic disturbances, and the like, can make fulfillment of a contract impossible, or severely delay its completion. Include *force majeure* provisions in your contracts.

### FORCE PROJECTION

An indirect pressure ploy.

Unions use force projection in contract negotiations. They hold a mass march to be seen by the managers. A disturbance, a few arrests, TV coverage of a police baton charge, or a fiery speech all contribute to force projection (in this case, of determination).

Buyers' force-projection measures include the following:

- Open contact with competition
- Competitors' letterhead visible on desk
- In-house costings in "make or buy" report
- Circular letter calling for tenders
  Seller's force-projection measures include these:
- Surcharges on small orders
- Lengthy delivery dates
- Publicity about growing market share
- Acquisition of, or merger with, rivals

All force-projection measures aim to influence the negotiators' EXPECTATIONS.

### FORMULA BARGAINING

An analytical approach to international diplomacy that divides negotiation into three phases:

- Prenegotiation or "diagnostic" phase
- Definition or "formula" phase
- "Detail" phase.

Negotiators are advised to do the following:

- Pay attention to the facts, the history of the problem, and how it has evolved.
- Look for precedents and how referents governing similar situations have developed.
- Know about the specific contexts and perceptions of the disputants and how they perceive their INTERESTS.

The negotiators search for a mutually acceptable formula that contains these elements:

- An agreed-on definition of the conflict
- Cognitive referents that imply a solution
- Some criterion of justice

Negotiators must remember that the problem, not the other party, is the "enemy" to be overcome.

The detail phase of the negotiations is a hard slog through the itemized applications of the formula.

Care is needed to do the following:

- Keep the "big picture" in focus while negotiating the details.
- Match flexibility with steadfastness in pursuit of clearly defined objectives.
- Handle the "eyeball-to-eyeball" moments in major international negotiations where there is a knife edge between success and resort to other options.

### FRIENDSHIP

Neither necessary nor sufficient to get an AGREEMENT, but seldom a hindrance.

The personal relationships of the negotiators can be warmer than the relationships between the constituents they represent. This is not an uncommon experience in difficult (for example, peace treaty) negotiations.

Working on the interpersonal relationship can help, but in some contexts it can hinder. For example, negotiating with officials from a bureaucracy can lead to misunderstandings if your friendly gestures are interpreted as enticing them into corrupt or disloyal stances. Certainly being on good terms with the other side is better than being barely able to speak to them. Remember, however, the exploitation of the friendship is not all one way (they get to you too).

### FRONTAL ASSAULT

A high-risk ploy to compromise the other negotiator's credibility. Typical frontal-assault statements:

- That is not what your predecessor said to us last time we met.

- Perhaps you should adjourn and consult with your people in more detail before you dig in too deep on this issue.

The other negotiator is irritated by this ploy and may blow his or her top. It could sour your relationship for good: use rarely.

## Game theory

Mathematical formulation of conflict dilemmas applied to the **BARGAINING** problem.

Game theory relies on key **ASSUMPTIONS**:

- The identity of the players and their number are fixed and known to everyone (you are not playing against the anonymous "market").

- All players are rational and everybody knows they are rational.

- The payoffs to each player are known.

- Each player's strategy is known and fixed.

The manipulation of available information for personal advantage between the players is limited, but not excluded, by the assumptions.

Two-person **ZERO SUM** games show that players in a pure conflict game assume that the other person is malevolent and therefore disposed to "do his or her worst" whatever **STRATEGY** is selected. A player does best by selecting the strategy that ensures the "best of the worst outcomes."

Two-person **NONZERO SUM** games are more complex. The degree of strategic interaction increases dramatically as the players explore opportunities for mutual gain. (See **NASH SOLUTION; PRISONER'S DILEMMA**)

## Generosity

Not contagious without a high degree of **TRUST** between the negotiators. Making unconditional offers does not promote reciprocal **GOODWILL**. The other negotiators perceive you to be in a weaker position, and revise their initial demands accordingly.

Unless and until you develop a strong relationship with the other negotiator, be like Scrooge rather than like St. Francis of Assisi. Where there is a long-term relationship, generosity can be a useful negotiating technique, as in the case of a husband and wife who have children and are negotiating the terms of a divorce.

### GETTING OUT FROM UNDER

Deals go sour. If you are in the pit, stop digging; get out from under.

We hang on in the hope that something will turn up. To give up is a defeat, a sign of weakness, a confession of failure. Right? Wrong.

Digging in when we have clearly made a mistake is for dummies.

If you cannot avoid the occasional lemon, get rid of it. After you have got out from under, study why you got into the mess in the first place.

### GETTING PAID

Not everyone gets paid what they are due. Getting paid is sometimes more difficult than doing the work you have not been paid for.

There can be genuine differences of opinion as to a number of factors:

- How much is owed
- What the agreed-on PRICE was
- Who was responsible for the revisions and variations
- The quality of the completed work

There are also failures to pay based on avoiding payment for wholly unscrupulous reasons.

Well-structured variation procedures identify the obligation to pay, and disciplined invoicing systems collect your money. (See CREDIT CONTROL)

### GIVE AND TAKE

A description of the negotiator's trading behavior. A caveat:

- "Giving" does not cause "getting."
- "Taking" does not cause "giving."

Trading requires linked give and take — one goes with the other. Therefore offer to give only if you simultaneously get something back in exchange.

### GO-BETWEEN

Trade name for someone akin to an AGENT, particularly in the Middle East.

A go-between is usually a national of the importing country who acts as the contact person between you and the importer. It is not always clear exactly for whom the go-between acts, but several countries insist that foreigners do all their business through a local one. In exchange for handling the transactions between the parties, the go-between receives a COMMISSION paid by the foreigner out of his or her share of the transaction.

As go-betweens often also act for the other party, or at least are candid with the other party about your limits, they can hardly be described as bona fide agents. Their status is inescapably ambiguous. Casual recruitment of a go-between can prove expensive. Consult your embassy's commercial attaché before embarking on a contract with a go-between.

### GOOD COP/BAD COP

A ploy that works best on frightened negotiators. It is an act: two negotiators alternate between a tough, uncompromising, highly aggressive, COMPETITIVE STYLE, and a softer, more COOPERATIVE STYLE.

Naturally you prefer to deal with the apparently softer negotiators, but their "hands are tied" by their tougher colleagues. They want to help you but they need you to help them. So you move closer to their position than you intended, but you are comforted by the illusion that this is a lot less far than you would have had to go to satisfy the "gorilla" who did all the shouting and made all those impossible demands.

You have been had. The duet was a setup to make you concede. Neither one is nicer or nastier than the other. They compare notes afterward, and laugh all the way to the next negotiation.

### GOODWILL

Earned but not given automatically.

Conceding something, no matter how little, in order to create goodwill is futile. The other negotiators stiffen their position when you make unconditional offers. Also, the "little" things you give away may acquire considerable leverage potential later in the negotiation — they could even clinch the AGREEMENT if offered at the right time — and throwing them away in the futile hope of creating goodwill is extremely costly when the result is that you have nothing left with which to close the deal.

### GREED

Snatching **DEADLOCK** out of the jaws of compromise by being too greedy.

You do not intend to be greedy, only ambitious. The other negotiator resents your greed and resists. You end up with nothing.

### GRIEVANCE

A major complaint. Do not just state a grievance, propose a remedy.

Concentrate your attention on your grievance and you are likely to argue. Think about what you want done about your grievance, and select a proportionate remedy within the other negotiator's limits (beware of **GREED**), and you are likely to enjoy the remedy sooner than you will settle an **ARGUMENT**.

### GROSS

The gross of anything is larger than the **NET**.

A percentage of gross income is worth more than a percentage of gross profit, and both are worth more than a percentage of net income or net profit, respectively. Especially true when the other negotiator controls the calculation of the net.

### GUARANTEE

Of great value where the risks of noncompliance are high. Banks take guarantees to cover their loans; clients want guarantees to cover your performance (see **PERFORMANCE BOND**); you like guarantees when it's your money at stake.

◻ Make sure, when giving guarantees, that you can pay up if things go wrong (Murphy's Law is no joke).

❐ Extravagant guarantees are dangerous.

❐ Ask for guarantees.

❐ If the other parties cannot guarantee something, adjust the PRICE downward.

❐ If they guarantee something as a matter of course, ask for a price without the guarantee (you are paying for it in an insurance premium anyway).

❐ If the guarantee needs to be invoked, consider a payment in lieu of litigation to collect it.

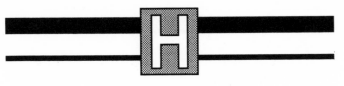

## HAGGLE

A noble art. The seller discovers the maximum a buyer will pay, without disclosing the minimum he or she will accept (and vice versa).

Haggling is part theater. Effective hagglers have a number of skills:

- They give plausible reasons for you to improve your **OFFER.**
- They rely on sympathy, emotions, their "facts," and your lack of stamina.
- They use mutual convergence between their current prices and yours to secure an **AGREEMENT.**
- They use silence effectively while waiting for you to move.
- They enter high/low to create room for them to move more slowly in smaller steps toward you than you move in larger steps toward them.

### HAVING IT BOTH WAYS

Negotiators often do, if you let them. For example, an increase in rent of $100 is an "intolerable burden"; an **OFFER** of $100 as a pay increase is an "insult."

*Counter:* Draw attention to the inconsistency, but remember that negotiators believe what they want to believe.

### HEADS OF AGENDA

A useful device — a listing of the issues — to get stalled talks restarted.

Your differences with the other side could be sharp. Perhaps you find it impossible to do the following:

- Handle all the differences
- Decide which issues should be tackled first
- Choose which issues should be tackled at all
- Separate out the poisoned relations between the parties

Try for a draft agenda that does not contain proposals and requires no explanation. Agree on a set of headings of the issues you want to discuss. These need not be placed in any particular order. If you can agree on even a restricted list of headings, this could precipitate enough momentum to allow the negotiations to recommence.

### HOOKER'S PRINCIPLE

Services are valued more highly before they are performed than they are afterward. When, for instance, does a plumber's fee look reasonable? When you are up to your knees in water.

Always agree on the basis under which you expect to be paid before you do the work. The buyers are more likely to pay during a crisis than they are when it has passed.

### HOSPITALITY

Welcome but dangerous. Hospitality exposes you to CONCESSION by obligation. Hospitality is a part of the furniture of social relationships. To refuse hospitality could be unhelpful. To partake, especially at an overly generous level (and your host controls the level), could imply obligations that you did not intend and raises QUESTIONS from your side about your objectivity.

Hospitality can be used to

- weaken your resolve;
- undermine your stamina (late nights, heavy drinking);
- trap you into indiscretion.

It can also be a genuine expression of a desire to do business together. How do you know which it is? Follow some rules.

❐ Insist on a reciprocity of equivalents: each side is hospitable to the other on the same basis.

❐ Do not compete on the level of hospitality.

❐ Do not socialize late every night (they have a supply of people to keep you at it, while their negotiators rest).

❐ Strictly limit your consumption of food, drink, and tobacco.

❐ Schedule your own caucus sessions for most evenings so that you can refuse an invitation without offense.

❐ Insist that "both sides bear their own costs."

❐ Cut out business lunches (they are mostly unproductive, expensive, and disruptive of the afternoon's schedules).

❐ Negotiate in working hours only.


### HOSTAGE NEGOTIATION

Hostages are taken either for material gain (cash) or political influence (publicity, revenge, humbling of an enemy, recognition, release of prisoners, change in policies). Terrorist extortion produces a common dilemma: if the demands are conceded, a spate of imitations can be expected; if the demands are not met, the hostages could be harmed.

Governments are less likely to concede to demands for political influence than they are to demands for material gains.

Terrorists implicitly concede that the government has higher humanitarian standards than their own, irrespective of the rhetoric that justifies their actions, for terrorism is only "successful" if the target is more concerned about the welfare of the victims than is the terrorist. This is a paradox for those terrorizing "evil" governments.

The government is constrained by public reaction to its behavior during a hostage incident.

- If it gives in to save lives, it cannot protect society from terrorist violence.

- If it refuses any deals with the terrorists, resulting in harm to the victims, it fails to protect citizens from the terrorists.

- If it attempts a physical rescue that also harms the victims, it is incompetent.

The government, not the terrorists, is usually put on trial by the media. The INTERESTS of the victims (survival) differ from those of both the terrorists and the government. Behavior conducive to survival is also the best STRATEGY: a victim has no option. Advice about handling the role of victim includes the following:

- Keep a low profile.

- Show no dissent.

- Do not argue with their beliefs.

- Do not attack them.

- Express no views.
- Show no impatience at all.

If the hostage group is small enough (a dozen or fewer), there is a possibility that the Stockholm syndrome will emerge — that is, a bonding relationship will develop between the terrorists and the victims. This can save lives. But making friends with the terrorists in a larger group is dangerous if the situation turns sour. They need someone to execute to increase their commitment, and if they shoot their friends, clearly they will shoot hostile strangers.

Choosing to negotiate with hostage takers involves these objectives:

- The release of the victims unharmed
- The failure of the terrorists to extract concessions of substance
- Dissuasion of imitators

Prevention of terrorism is preferable to curing it; but failing prevention, what are the options?

The terrorists reinforce commitment by threatening to kill hostages. Initially, they set out their demands (which, if ludicrously high, imply irrational and probably unstable people, and if very low, imply media manipulators). They demand to communicate with high officials, they demand publicity, they set deadlines. Either the deadlines are extended or the terrorists implement their threats.

The government should leave negotiations to the security forces. It is best that the official in communication with the terrorists is, or is perceived to be, of lowly rank. Time is required to find out about the hostage takers (to choose the most appropriate psychological approach) and to plan intervention by force.

The terrorists do not know for certain which policy the government is pursuing, so they impose short deadlines. They are constrained by the fact that shooting victims reduces the value of their threats (and gives the security forces a publicly acceptable reason for intervening by force).

Government tactics include the following:

- Using TIME and isolation in tandem to undermine the terrorists' resolve to continue
- Doing nothing in a hurry, no matter what the THREAT, right from the start
- Doing everything possible to increase the feeling of normality in the immediate vicinity (do not close the airport; its continued functioning helps undermine the terrorists' feeling of self-importance)

Here the media could help (but seldom do). Mentioning the incident occasionally helps, saturation coverage does not. (Not mentioning it at all for a day or so would be best.)

Condemning the incident in public undermines the ploy of isolation, and allowing ministers to visit the scene is absolutely counterproductive.

In summary:

- Isolate the incident.
- Downplay its significance.
- Curtail (by self-denial) media coverage.
- Engage in negotiations at a low level.
- Make no moves in response to acts of violence.
- Maintain flexibility of means to achieve firmly set goals.

Remember, winning a hostage crisis is seldom an option (the fact that it occurs is a victory for the terrorists), and your overall OBJECTIVE is to minimize the costs of concluding it without encouraging repetition.

### HOTEL PURCHASE

Valuations of hotels are based on their income-earning capacities. One guide is the annual revenue (GROSS if selling; NET of taxes if buying). Revenue shows the recent trade of the hotel — what it actually does — not what it could do under your management. If there are unusual considerations producing recent revenues, these influence the PRICE.

If buying a hotel from a conglomerate, be wary of inflated revenue figures. Other divisions of the conglomerate could be under instruction to use the hotel services. Once the hotel is sold to you, these purchases are no longer available.

When buying a hotel from a liquidator, be wary of the current trading accounts. The liquidator keeps the hotel open to sell it as a "going concern," and therefore slashes all expenditures to the bone. This reduces cost of sales, and makes the potential profit look better than it is. Repairs and maintenance, even cleaning, can be suspended for a short period.

Base your OFFER on annual sales plus stock at valuation (SAV). If you do not want the stock, or any part of it (check all "sell by" dates on booze and supplies), separate it out and require its disposal. Consider changing brewers to avoid paying for unsold previous stocks.

Try for CONTINGENCY PRICING if you doubt the figures.

If there are disposables (valuable furniture, spare land,

spare buildings, associated rights), can you sell them to reduce the cost of purchase? (Do not disclose your intentions; the seller could apply your ideas.)

### Hustle close

A pressure tactic:

- This plane is leaving right now. It costs four ounces of gold for the last seat, or you learn Arabic.
- You know you'll never get a better deal than this one. If you don't take it right now, I'll hang up and call my lawyers.

*Counter:* Compare the OFFER against your options. If better, take it; if worse, do not (see BATNA).

### "I AM ONLY A SIMPLE GROCER"

A disarming ploy to relax negotiators into indiscretions about their objectives, tactics, and hidden intentions. You think you are dealing with a novice because he (or she) claims to be "only a simple grocer," but in reality you are dealing with the owner of the world's largest grocery chain.

### IF

A negotiator's most useful two-letter word. All proposals should start with "if" to tell them what they must do for you if you are to do something for them. If they reject your conditions, you are free to amend, postpone, or withdraw your PROPOSAL. (See WHAT IF?)

### IMPASSE

When disagreement has been reached in direct negotiations and further negotiations seem impossible. Often a mediator is called in at this stage to assist the parties — sometimes voluntarily by ad hoc agreement of both parties, and sometimes by law, as in U.S. labor law. A good mediator begins by trying to discover the nature of the impasse and moves on from there to assist the parties in bridging the gap.

### IMPORTS

Without them we would be poorer (see EXPORTS).

Issues to negotiate with your supplier (the exporting company) include the following:

❑ Who bears the foreign exchange RISK?

❑ Who bears the cost of credit?

❑ Which PRICE prevails: ex-factory, cost, insurance and freight (CIF), free on board (FOB)?

❑ How is the exporter paid?

### "I'M SORRY, I'VE MADE A MISTAKE"

A seller's ploy, close to the ETHICS border. A seller calls you back and apologizes because she has quoted a price from an outdated version of her catalog. Instead of the product costing $4.55 each, it is listed in the new catalog at $4.95 each. The mistake was revealed when she placed your order for 1,000 units. She cannot sell them at $4.55 because her boss will not authorize it. Her explanation is punctuated with profuse apologies.

If you believe the seller to be genuine, you agree to the higher PRICE. If you do not, cancel the order. This depends on how important the price mistake was against the total price, and how easy it is to find another seller. Most times buyers succumb, albeit reluctantly, to the ploy.

### INCENTIVE

Motivating by carrot. Offer an incentive for measurable performance and people respond. Supplying incentive gifts (a euphemism for expensive staff presents) is a thriving business.

### INDEMNITY

Expensive to buy; risky to do without.

Your professional advice puts you at RISK if someone fouls up as a result of acting on it. Indemnity insurance protects you against malpractice claims.

The premiums are high because malpractice awards are high; because they are high, they are rife; they are rife because claimants are imaginative; claimants are imaginative because lawyers encourage claims to increase the awards; to reduce the awards, insurers face high costs; because of the awards and high costs to insurers, the premiums are high.

The concept of unlimited liability for professional advisers was meant to concentrate their minds on the advisability of proffering advice.

### INFORMATION

Can help or hinder your negotiations.

Information about the other party can be valuable — for example, when you discover how badly they need your cooperation. Conversely, disclosing your own needs can damage your stance.

### INHIBITIONS

Concerns that prevent you from agreeing to a **PROPOSAL**. You must decide whether to present your inhibitions openly to the other side and insist that they be addressed or leave them unexpressed when presenting proposals that address them. This approach conceals your prejudices.

Listening to what people say reveals their inhibitions.

- They do not trust you.
- They are worried about precedent.
- They need to be paid quickly.
- They want to be more selective than the law allows (sexism, racism, ageism, and so on).
- They are frightened of publicity.

- They do not know if it works.

  Your proposals should address their inhibitions.

### INTEGRATIVE BARGAINING

Searching for solutions to problems when the negotiators have compatible INTERESTS.

By emphasizing the commonality of interests in CONFLICT situations, integrative bargaining can reformulate distributive ZERO SUM disputes into integrative NON-ZERO SUM possibilities.

Integrative bargaining can lead to PROBLEM SOLVING. Considerable TRUST both in you and in the process is required (earned, not assumed).

A mixture of integrative and DISTRIBUTIVE BARGAINING is more likely to be successful than is an approach based totally on one or the other.

### INTEREST RATE

The PRICE of money. This varies widely for several purposes:

- To cover for the opportunity cost of money (how much you can get in an alternative lending activity)
- To cover for the RISK involved
- To reflect its scarcity value for you (how badly do you want the money?)

### INTERESTS

Why you prefer some things to others. Your interests motivate your wants. Interests may be hidden because you are

- unaware of them;
- embarrassed by them;
- confusing them with your wants.

To uncover interests, ask why they want what they are demanding. Is there some other way that you can satisfy their interests?

When our interests are in conflict with our feelings we face a difficult choice.

Interest-based negotiations take a different approach from POSITIONAL BARGAINING. In the former, "interests" become translated into "concerns" — objectives related to the particular issue at hand — which are not to be confused with "positions."

### INTERPERSONAL ORIENTATION

Psychological insight into how people interact. Negotiators operate along a continuum. They have a high interpersonal orientation if they are responsive to other people. They have a low interpersonal orientation if they prefer to be uninvolved with what is happening to others.

When both negotiators have high interpersonal orientation, they

- engage in cooperative behavior;
- are likely to solve problems;
- have warm personal relations.

A negotiator with low interpersonal orientation

- aims to gain as much as he can without consideration of the other's behavior;
- does not take anything personally;

- believes that the balance of **POWER** pushes others to behave competitively or cooperatively (out of confidence or desperation);
- works for his own **INTERESTS**;
- does not react to the other's behavior;
- exploits a cooperative stance;
- expects other negotiators to look after their own interests and to be the best judge of them;
- is not the best team member in delicate and sensitive negotiations;
- is useful in the early stages of a difficult negotiation (cease-fire, arms control, exchange of prisoners);
- is not useful if relationships need to be warmed;
- offends some negotiators and causes breakdowns that have nothing to do with the substantive issues.

And when both negotiators have low interpersonal orientations, they

- aim to maximize their own interests;
- delay settlement because their moves are based only on self-interest;
- do not generate bonds of **TRUST**.

### INTIMIDATION

Can be overt (bullying, gangsterism) or covert (self-induced).

Covert intimidation is more widespread but hardly noticeable. It works almost entirely through your own mind.

Covert intimidation operates through the power of suggestion. It is the ultimate untested assumption.

People covertly intimidate because it works.

**INTIMIDATOR**

You may never know you have been intimidated covertly, but watch out for well-worn intimidators such as these:

❑ Uncomfortable seating, lower than the intimidator's

❑ Poorly positioned seating — in a draft, facing the sun or its reflection, or in front of an open door through which other people can hear your conversation

❑ You are kept waiting.

During the negotiation intimidators may do one or more of the following:

❑ Take phone calls, speak to secretaries and colleagues, and look at their watches

❑ Tell somebody they will be free in a few minutes when you have just started

❑ Complain about your products or services and your company

❑ Praise the competition and appear to know all your rivals by their first names (they keep forgetting yours)

❑ Appear inattentive or not interested in anything you say

❑ Ignore your literature, fail to answer QUESTIONS or state their needs, and appear generally indifferent.

Intimidators are not rude, they are at work on your perceptions. They aim to force you to move further toward their targets than you intended.

## KIDNAP NEGOTIATION

Kidnappers coerce their targets by threatening to harm their victims. Kidnapping poses different problems from that of hostage taking.

- The kidnapper's lair is not known.
- The police are not deployed outside it.
- The kidnappers choose and prepare their location.
- The kidnappers choose when to communicate with the target.
- The police cannot manipulate the environment to isolate the kidnappers.
- The kidnappers do not seek publicity.
- The kidnappers can rest at will.
- The kidnappers choose whether to continue extortion or quit (about 20% of kidnap victims are killed).

The target must decide whether to involve the authorities or to meet the kidnapper's demands. While an individual can be intimidated into ignoring a crime, the state cannot.

Kidnappers are vulnerable during the handover of the ransom because they have to reveal where and when to do so. Laws prohibit the paying of ransom and the entire assets of a target can be frozen to prevent it. These laws can be circumvented if the target has resources outside their jurisdiction and can pay without revealing the details to the authorities.

Targets have to be sure they are dealing with the people who actually hold the victim, because some callers will be bogus (you can use code words). If interlopers have solved the handover problem, but do not hold the victim, they could get paid by you for nothing. Evidence that the victim is alive or the property is intact (for example, photographs containing today's newspaper) can be demanded in return for cooperation, but most evidence is unreliable and, anyway, may be refused.

The authorities are particularly unhappy about those organizations that insure the ransom fee and even arrange to negotiate with the kidnappers and pay up. This form of antikidnapping "insurance" goes into effect without incriminating contact between the insurers and the target. Of course, knowledge of a target who is both vulnerable to kidnapping and has insurance coverage is surely a temptation to potential kidnappers.

### Killer line

The killer lines that put you on the spot include these:

- You'll have to do better than that.
- Give me your best PRICE.

One sentence gets them a major CONCESSION, so they will probably try a few more killers to see just how soft you are on price. In fact, you may be bidding downward against yourself.

*Counter:* Seek more information.

- What other proposals have they received?
- Is it APPLES AND ORANGES?
- If they have a better price, why don't they take it?

Either there is something in your proposal they like, which means it is worth its price, or they are fishing with a price challenge. Think about your reaction to killer lines.

## KILLER QUESTIONS

Questions to put you on the spot. Answer yes or no and you could be in trouble. For example: "Is that your final OFFER?" "Yes" ends the negotiation. "No" tells the other negotiators that you have other (better for them) proposals.

Their next question is going to be: "Well, what is your final offer? Is that PROPOSAL negotiable?" "Yes" opens the negotiation on your next proposal. "No" ends the negotiation.

*Counter:* "My proposal is based on the circumstances as I understand them at present, but I am always willing to listen to constructive suggestions that will improve the acceptability of my proposal."

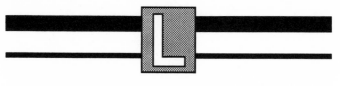

## Last clear chance

A method to apportion blame for an incident (e.g., STRIKE, lawsuit, failure to supply). Even if both parties contribute to it, the one with the last clear chance to prevent it is culpable. If you have the last clear chance to avert the incident, you have the unenviable choice of backing off or causing it.

## Law

Best observed, especially when inconvenient.

The rule of law is preferred to the rule of men. For every victim of an unjust law, there are many more victims of unjust conduct. Without the rule of law:

- contracts would be unenforceable;
- property rights would be meaningless;
- promises need not be kept;
- threats would be arbitrary;
- lives would be in jeopardy.

## Lease

An alternative to ownership.

Consider the following points when negotiating a lease AGREEMENT.

❑ Who are the parties to the agreement?

❑ Is there a declaration of nonnominee status? If falsely declared, the property reverts with no compensation and without prejudice to money owed.

❑ Who is guaranteeing the lessee's obligations? If lessee fails to meet obligations, the reversion clause applies.

- What exactly is being leased?
- How much is the rent?
- When it is paid (in advance or arrears, monthly, quarterly)?
- Is there a premium and on what basis? For the "fixtures and fittings," for the "availability" of the lease?
- When does the lease commence?
- How long is it for?
- Can it be extended and on whose initiative?
- When are rent reviews scheduled and are they only upward?
- What criteria apply: cost of living, valuation, yield of similar properties?
- How are disputes settled?
- Is there a "rent-free" period and for how long?
- Who pays other charges during this period?
- What service charges is the lessee liable for?
- Who pays the rates/charges?
- Is it a "full repairs and insurance" lease?
- What access does the lessor have for inspections?
- Who specifies the extent of repairs and choice of contractor?
- Can lessee sublet?
- With lessor's consent ("not unreasonably withheld")?
- Within what duration of the lease (rent-review period only)?
- Can lessee assign lease with or without lessor's consent?
- On what terms can lessee surrender the lease?

◻ Who pays legal costs of the transaction?

◻ What obligations does tenant have to planning regulations?

◻ If new regulations are applied during the tenancy, who pays for them?

◻ What obligations does tenant have to the building's fixtures and fittings and to their care and upkeep?

◻ What notification must lessee give of intention to make any alterations to the building?

◻ What regulations must lessee apply? These may include

◻     requirements for fire certificates;

      prohibitions on storing dangerous or toxic chemicals;

      prohibitions on specified dangerous or illegal (or disreputable?) activities;

      compliance with all laws on occupation and use;

      limitations on official cubic space per person employed;

      city ordinance requiring lessees to refrain from causing a nuisance or obstruction of any kind.

◻ Reversion clause to apply for serious or persistent minor breaches at lessor's discretion.

### LENDABILITY FACTOR

A subjective judgment (by the lender, not by you) of the following:

• Your character: are you to be trusted with the lender's money?

• Your record: what your recent past shows.

- Your proposition: what the money is to be used for (how it increases your NET WORTH).
- Your terms: what is in it for the lender?

### LETTER OF CREDIT (LOC)

Facilitates foreign trade; terms are negotiable.

If you are exporting, require the importer to open a credit line with your bank for the value of the goods, CIF or FOB, with the following features:

- Confirmed: importer's bank guarantees payment on production of appropriate shipping documents.
- Irrevocable: prevents importer from refusing payment on a pretext.
- Transferable: enables you to endorse it for other transactions.
- Divisible: for partial payments on other deals.

If you are importing, require the exporter to accept a letter of credit.

- Make it payable when the goods have passed your inspection (is revocable).
- Trade this for transferability and divisibility, which are direct benefits to the payee.

Practice varies and reflects the balance of POWER. The wording of an LOC is absolutely crucial, and should be scrutinized carefully. A glance at disputes in case law over LOCs should keep you awake at night.

### LEVEL UP THE WORK, LEVEL DOWN THE PRICE

No two bids are the same except through collusion. Each includes different commitments and features.

Select the commitments and features you prefer. This

is your "leveled-up work specification." Ask the suppliers to reoffer the leveled-up specification at or below the lowest priced quotation. This is your leveled-down price.

Some suppliers may not rebid. Others may rebid and move up on PRICE. If anyone rebids and meets the leveled-down price, consider awarding them the contract (but beware of BLOCKING BID).

### LEVERAGE

Bargaining power: it is important to know what leverage you have, even if you choose not to apply it.

Almost anything that you have discretion over gives you leverage. Who has leverage?

- Air-traffic controllers at Thanksgiving (or any holiday, for that matter).
- Construction workers when a project is time-critical.
- Exhibition workers when the exhibition is due to open.
- Stagehands just before the show.
- Advertisers when TV channels have spare slots.
- TV channels when prime-time slots are full.

*Counters:* Not easy to counter or it would not be leverage. Raise the stakes.

- Fire the air-traffic controllers.
- Cancel the event.
- Lock out strikers for twice as long as they strike.
- Ban advertisers for six months.
- Switch channels, or media.
  Lower the stakes.

- Reward negotiators who do not apply leverage unfairly.
- Negotiate other than when leverage can be applied.
- Do not exploit own leverage.
- Reward advertisers who pay full rates with prime-time preference slots.
- Reward TV channels that give preference to off-peak bookings.

### LIFEBOAT CLAUSE

When you need a lifeboat, you need a lifeboat. For protection when buying, add this clause to your AGREEMENT: ". . . this offer is contingent on the veracity of all statements made by the seller in respect of the proposed sale, including all statements regarding performance, quality, availability and specifications, and approval of the buyer of all matters relevant to the purchase, whether presently known or not, and any other material facts that may affect the buyer's interests."

You now have an unlimited exit should you find it in your INTERESTS to jump into a lifeboat.

### LIFETIME COSTS

Forget them at your peril. Remember, the acquisition cost is only part of the PRICE. How much does it cost to maintain the purchased item or service?

### LINKING

Opens up bargaining possibilities.

Presented with a list of demands, or an OFFER with more than one element, do you deal with each issue separately by treating each one as a distinct mininegotiation? Or do you link them together on the basis that "nothing is agreed until everything is agreed"?

Separating the issues has one advantage: it narrows down the remaining items in dispute. This blocks off obstructive ploys by parties who hold out for concessions in one area favorable to them for agreement in other areas favorable to others.

Separating the issues has disadvantages, however. The outstanding issues are normally highly contentious (that is why they are outstanding). This leaves very little room for movement. The settled issues may have been settled "too quickly," curtailing opportunities for additional movement. By separating the issues, you could be restricting yourself when you come to deal with the contentious items.

By linking the issues, you negotiate to where you can get an **AGREEMENT**, but any agreement is "subject to agreement on all the issues." Linking is more complex to conduct than single-issue **BARGAINING**. **SUMMARIZING** skills are valuable at any time, but they are at a premium in a linked negotiation.

## Liquidity

Highly desirable when you need it, expensive when you do not.

Assets have varying degrees of liquidity. Cash is instant liquidity, but it has drawbacks:

- · It does not earn interest.
- Holding large sums is expensive in foregone earnings.
- It is risky (vulnerable to thieves, fire, flood, carelessness).

Money in a bank with instant access during banking hours is as good as cash. Electronic tellers give 24 hours' liquidity at ATMs or by signal to whatever country has open at that moment banks in which the payee has an account.

### LISTENING

Most important skill of the successful negotiator.

It could be the only CONCESSION the other negotiators require: they want someone to listen to their views, respect them and take account of them. They may not expect more than that.

The message sent is often not the message received. People are poor listeners. Even if the message is heard clearly, recall deteriorates rapidly as TIME passes.

Listening to what a negotiator says is hard work. Experiments show how difficult it is to recall accurately even vivid messages, let alone routine ones.

Here are some tips to improve your listening.

❑ Ask QUESTIONS for clarification.

❑ Summarize the statements to the satisfaction of the speaker.

❑ Do not interrupt.

❑ Avoid composing your rejection of what other parties are saying before they finish saying it.

❑ Cease anticipating what they are about to say (you miss the surprises).

❑ Do not judge the message by the messenger.

❑ Treat the other party's statements with respect.

❑ Avoid reacting emotionally to views you find distasteful or disagreeable.

Here are some tips to help those who listen to you.

❑ Speak clearly and for short periods only.

❑ Summarize your points.

❑ Answer questions briefly.

❑ Avoid diluting your stronger points with weaker points that divert attention from your main message.

## Loan

Against **COLLATERAL**, a loan can be worthwhile.

It makes sense to borrow other people's money for wealth-creating purposes only (see **NET WORTH**); it never makes sense to borrow, or to lend, for income.

## Lockout

Management's answer to a **STRIKE**. The company refuses work for its employees until certain conditions are met: a return to "normal working," for example, or a willingness to undertake specified duties.

Disruptive union tactics can be countered by a lockout. A union may pursue disruptive tactics for the following reasons:

• Its leaders are not sure of the support for an all-out strike.

• It can levy those who continue to work to compensate those who are sent home without pay for carrying out union instructions.

• It can prolong a dispute for months, causing more problems for the company than for union members.

Should the company impose costs on the employees by sending the entire work force home? Yes, if this is likely to force a more realistic negotiating stance on the union. No, if the dispute slides into intransigence (see **MARTYRDOM**).

Alternatively, can the firm cope by adapting to the loss of key staff and thus isolate those whose labor has been withdrawn?

### LOSE-LOSE

It happens: neither party can find a compromise, either because each insists that only the other move, or because there is no settlement range in the respective positions.

Insisting on winning means both lose.

### Major sacrifice gambit

A ploy that manipulates the perceptions of the other negotiators.

Having decided on a traded CONCESSION, you refer to its "significance" and build it up as a major concession as credibly as you can.

If the other side believes you, it might offer another concession on another issue. Suggest an area where it can compensate you for your "heroic" sacrifice.

### Management fees

An alternative to the ownership of capital assets, which are at RISK of expropriation, destruction, and deterioration.

Propose a contract to manage assets on the owner's behalf, or to provide a service that the client prefers not to supply. Fee income is calculated on "what the market will bear," consistent with a minimum level to cover actual costs.

The benefits include

- not having large capital projects at risk;
- not having to fund them.

Your net earnings can be equivalent to your earnings from owning and operating the capital commitment.

From the owner's point of view, the drawbacks include:

- vulnerability to the managers' setting a fee structure that you cannot audit for value;
- reducing funds available for depreciation if the negotiated fee exceeds the expected profit from the assets;

- the risk of departure by the professional managers — leaving inefficiently managed assets — if you reduce the negotiated fee.

The owner's **STRATEGY** is to acquire expertise in managing by training local people and to reduce fees to competitive rates by issuing tenders for the contract.

## MANDATE

Defines and limits your authority.

Discretion is a heavy but avoidable responsibility. If you exceed your mandate, your deal could be repudiated.

Employees limit the discretion of their representatives by mandating them not to accept any **PROPOSAL** without their approval, and not to accept anything less than the mandated demand. This is often a ploy to enhance commitment rather than an immovable stance.

How can you handle a mandate demand? Not by conceding it, unless you want to receive more of the same (see **SKINNER'S PIGEON**). If you believe it is a **COMMITMENT PLOY**, do not challenge the commitment; employees might demonstrate how strongly they feel committed. If the mandate is the true wish of the employees, treat their feelings firmly, though gently, and with a regard to your **INTERESTS**.

Not all mandate demands survive the first refusal.

## MARKET

All of the following descriptions apply to the market:
- It processes information about prices.
- It can be global or localized.
- It signals discrepancies in wants and the means to

meet them, and does so without central or any other kind of direction.

- It is resistant to interference (though not indefinitely).
- It is suppressible only in the short term.
- It is pervasive across language, cultural, and ethnic barriers.

The nature of markets creates the need for negotiation, for although the market signals a PRICE, that price is the result of infinite adjustments by people to their perceptions of demand and supply. Many of these adjustments are contradictory. People have a tendency to

❏ sell when they should hold on;

❏ buy when they should desist;

❏ do neither when they should do both.

The constant adjustment of the market, its impermanence for more than a moment, and its uncertainty about the future make negotiating its ideal instrument.

## MARTYRDOM

Never underestimate the ability of people to perform acts that are detrimental to their best INTERESTS. Do not assume that people rationally calculate the net benefits of a course of action.

Negotiators can react irrationally, even suicidally, to change. They know that they are going to lose, but their defiance is fed by their emotions. Martyrdom comforts the defiant, the desperate, and the dedicated, and for them this comfort far outweighs their sacrifice.

Theatening martyrs plays into their hands. They receive a new lease on life and public sympathy instead of being rejected as clowns.

Martyrs can be exasperating, dangerous, and expensive.

## MEDIATION

Shares a blurred boundary between ARBITRATION and negotiation.

Negotiators in DEADLOCK may seek a settlement that neither side can find a way to move toward. A mediator is a neutral third party who helps the disputing parties try to reach agreement.

Unlike the arbitrator, the mediator does not enforce movement. Unlike the negotiator, the mediator does not trade movement. The mediator first identifies what can be done and then informs each negotiator that there is a possibility of movement.

The mediator establishes whether there is a settlement range of which the parties are presently unaware. The mediator is not concerned with the justice of each negotiator's position, how "fair" or "reasonable" it is, or whether it corresponds to the "facts." However, he or she may caution the negotiators that their PROPOSAL contains serious obstacles. It remains the negotiators' responsibility whether to pursue a mediator's recommendations.

Mediators must
- take firm charge of the process of dispute settlement;
- be totally indifferent to the settlement;
- not deliberate or judge the merits of the issues;
- set the rules of the debate;
- not permit interruptions of what one person says ("your turn comes later");
- permit any option from the list of possible solutions

("no option is agreed on or rejected just because it is discussed");

- insist on no negotiation until all the views of each side have been expressed.

The mediator asks each side to verify to the other the basis of its facts and claims and to explain why its proposed solution should be acceptable.

Mediation may range from pure facilitation, in which the mediator refrains from any judgments about the merits of the issues, to more evaluative mediation wherein the mediator conveys to each side an evaluation of that side's strengths and weaknesses.

### MEMORANDUM OF UNDERSTANDING

Drawn up to commit the parties loosely before the details are agreed on. A memorandum of understanding (MOU) outlines the mutual understanding of the negotiators about their intentions to proceed to an AGREEMENT without binding them into an irreversible relationship.

Insert the statement "This MOU is subject to final contract," and see that it appears in all correspondence referring to the MOU.

### MINIMUM ORDER PLOY

Enhances the value of an order for the seller. Examples include the following:

- We only sell these in packs of six.
- If we represent you in the purchase of the building, we must also act as rental agents if you acquire it.

*Counter:* Test their seriousness by your certain choice of the alternative of no order at all.

### Mini-trial

Each side presents a shortened version of its position to a neutral facilitator (usually not a judge and jury), often with decision makers from both sides present. Often the decision makers have not previously heard each other's case except through their own lawyer's reports, and they have not seen their own position reacted to by the other side. Often a very useful device in moving parties from impasse to settlement.

### Minutes

Minutes record the following:
- Who was present during negotiation
- When and where the negotiation took place
- Brief notes on the AGENDA
- Summaries of each negotiator's main views
- Commitments to look at specific topics
- Proposals that are made
- Anything agreed on

Preparing the minutes of a discussion is not easy even if you are neutral; when you are one of the players, it is difficult to do to the complete satisfaction of the other negotiators. Do not succumb to the temptation to "bend" the minutes to suit your own INTERESTS. Others may fail to notice the alteration, but they are less likely to overlook the consequences. It is interesting that most mistakes in minutes are to the advantage of the side that prepared them.

### Mother hubbard

A PRICE pressure ploy implying "the cupboard is bare." Challenge the seller's price as follows:

- Assert your desire to buy, but convince the seller that your budget does not allow you to buy at the quoted price. Support this with evidence (for example, minutes of the budget meeting, written instructions).
- Block off all attempts to restructure your budget by running it over two periods and across different headings, introducing installments and "creative accounting."
- Place the onus of finding a way to reduce the price on the seller.

Close to a sale, the seller will search for ways of meeting your budget figure. Some of the changes may be

- cosmetic, but nevertheless valuable to you;
- "creative accounting" (in the seller's accounts, not yours);
- tangible to you (e.g., shifting the money to after-sales costs);
- a straight cut in price.

How far below the quoted price you aim your Mother Hubbard is a matter of judgment: too far and they break off; too close and you pay more than you need to (though any price cut is better than none).

*Counter:* Difficult if the cupboard is really bare. Try detailed questioning of the budget process and find where the authority to change it lies. It is better to be over the alleged budget because you have priced the "extras" as add-ons than over it with everything priced on an inclusive basis.

### Motivation

Other people's motives are baser than our own. This harmless delusion becomes dangerous when we act as if other negotiators respond only to the motivations we ascribe to them.

| Ascribed Motive | Competitive Action | Cooperative Action |
|---|---|---|
| Fear | Threaten | Assure |
| Pride | Mock | Flatter |
| Hatred | Hate | Love |
| Loyalty | Exploit | Reward |
| Money | Minimize | Maximize |
| Love | Withhold | Requite |
| Desire | Frustrate | Satisfy |
| Jealousy | Excite | Calm |
| Ambition | Block | Assist |

To assume that money is the only motivator of all employees ignores a whole range of other motivators, some of which, if recognized and attended to, might be cheaper than an elaborate pay reward system.

## MOU

See MEMORANDUM OF UNDERSTANDING

### MUTUAL GAINS BARGAINING

Win-win negotiations.

This model of negotiation assumes that people can be made to see their impasse as a problem to be solved, and that if everyone contributes to solving it there may well be gains for all involved, rather than one party winning and another losing. Mutual gains is probably a better phrase than WIN-WIN because *gains* can include moving toward something better, while *winning* implies that the parties are battling. Increasingly used as a model in U.S. labor/management negotiations.

## MUTUALITY PRINCIPLE

The union claims a mutual right with management to decide on certain issues. Union STRATEGY is to widen the areas of mutuality from conventional wages and working conditions to areas normally reserved to management.

Unions also seek to achieve mutuality on some older areas of managerial prerogatives such as promotion, selection, hiring, discipline, firing, and training.

### Nash solution

Economist's model of the bargaining problem.

Nash showed that faced with a choice of achieving some minimum outcome (their "security level") and incrementally improving on that level by accommodating each other, negotiators maximized the product of their incremental utilities. Nash's solution, by ASSUMPTIONS, abstracts from the skills and bargaining POWER of each individual.

### Needs theory

Meet a negotiator's needs and you are on your way toward agreement, says Gerard Nierenberg, who developed an approach that begins with Abraham Maslow's hierarchy of needs (see PSYCHOLOGY OF NEGOTIATION).

Nierenberg categorized six varieties of application ranked by the degree of control that negotiators may exercise over the outcome.

1. Negotiators working for the opposers' needs: assure, encourage, concede

2. Negotiators letting the opposers work for their own needs: motivate, permit, challenge

3. Negotiators working for the opposers' and their own needs: cooperate, compromise, recognize

4. Negotiators working against their own needs: waive, relinquish, disavow

5. Negotiators working against the opposers' needs: veto, embarrass, threaten

6. Negotiators working against the opposers' and their own needs: thwart, renounce, withdraw

Each need has an appropriate or potential tactic that can be applied to interpersonal, interorganizational, and diplomatic conflicts.

### NEED TO GO?

Negotiators who take work with them when traveling, especially abroad, should consider whether they will actually work on long journeys.

Travel is tiring. Will you open the file late in the evening and begin work? Should papers concerning other negotiations be risked in travel?

### NEED TO KNOW

Security in the negotiating team is a prudent precaution. Premature disclosure whether by accident or theft worsens your prospects of a deal.

Negotiating teams should take the following precautions:

❏ Prepare in secure premises.

❏ Adopt a numbering system for all documents and restrict their circulation.

❏ Brief senior personnel in person.

❏ Remember that only the negotiators need to see the briefs and the crucial data.

❏ Shred or otherwise destroy documents that are no longer needed.

❏ Enlist positive support for basic security measures from all negotiators involved.

❏ Screen the office staff and the service providers (e.g., cleaning-company employees).

❏ Relieve colleagues with known personal problems of involvement in a high-stress negotiation.

### NEGOTIATING LANGUAGE

Some types of language help a negotiator, particularly in the BARGAINING phase. "We require" is more assertive than "we would like," and it is more likely to get attention than a vague expression of desire.

Tell them what you want, and tell them what you are willing to TRADE with them to get it.

| Assertive Language | Weaker Language |
|---|---|
| I require | I would like |
| I need | I wish |
| I must | I hope |
| I want | I am in the mood for |
| I insist | I feel |

### NEGOTIATING SKILL

What distinguishes the above-average negotiator from the rest? Studies of negotiators have identified some of the characteristics of above-average negotiators. If the differences in performance can be replicated with training and practice, below-average negotiators can improve their performance.

Neil Rackham and John Carlisle concluded that the differences in performance were sufficiently consistent to be identified and that negotiating skills could be taught. They found that above-average negotiators tend to do the following:

- Explore more options
- Devote much more time to considering areas of potential agreement (though both types of negotiator spend most of their time considering differences)
- Spend twice as much time considering long-term is-

sues (though both types spend over 90% of their time on short-term issues)

- Set objectives within a range rather than at a fixed point
- Leave open the order in which they consider the issues during face-to-face contact
- Use far fewer irritators (self-praise for their own proposals) that do not persuade and are therefore counterproductive
- Make far fewer instant counterproposals
- Initiate far fewer defend/attack spirals
- Label their own behavior before proceeding ("Could I ask a question?"), although when in disagreement they give their reasons first and then state that they disagree
- Test their understanding more often
- Summarize more often
- Ask many more QUESTIONS
- Give more information about personal feelings
- Refrain from diluting arguments with weaker and more vulnerable statements
- Review the events that occurred during the negotiation

### NEGOTIATING WITH YOURSELF

A common enough activity. We perceive we are weaker than we really are and we lower our EXPECTATIONS. We anticipate how they are likely to react to our proposals, so we soften them. It is more fruitful to negotiate with the other party than ourselves; they may be negotiating with themselves instead.

### NET

Always smaller than GROSS, so be careful when negotiators refer to net amounts. The gross amount, less deductibles, equals the net amount. Deductibles are disputable. The share of a net sum, be it profit, income, or interest, is of uncertain value to the receiver and depends on the motives of the calculator. Offer net shares, but demand gross shares.

### NET WORTH

Deduct what you owe from what you own: this is your net worth. If it is negative, you are vulnerable. You prefer that your net worth is positive and rising.

### NEUTRAL EVALUATION

The parties agree to have a neutral third party hear both sides and provide an evaluation. This can be part of mediation. It can also be part of nonbinding arbitration, for the parties to accept or reject or to form the basis for further negotiations. U.S. courts are experimenting with requiring case evaluation by small juries, for example, as a way to move the parties toward settlement.

### NOAH'S ARK

A buyer's pressure ploy: "You'll have to do better than that because your rivals are quoting better prices than you are." It is almost always a bluff. Noah's Ark has been part of the buyer's repertoire of winning moves for so long that Noah let two of them on board.

Sometimes buyers do have a better PRICE; more often, however, they do not have comparable packages from the sellers (see APPLES AND ORANGES).

- Comparable packages but different prices. If you drop your price, the buyer is better off by the difference and can induce your rivals to follow suit against you (see **DUTCH AUCTION**).

- Noncomparable packages and therefore noncomparable prices. If you believe that the proposals are comparable and you reduce your price, the buyer is better off.

- Rivals' prices are higher (or you believe them to be). If you reduce your prices to defeat rivals (real or imagined), the buyer is better off.

Because Noah's Ark is beneficial to buyers, it is the most persistently used ploy in negotiations all over the world.

*Counters:* Question the buyer's comparisons, refuse to react unless you can compare the quotes directly, and ask why the buyer is dealing with you if rivals' quotes are better.

### No come-backs

The truly one-off deal. No warranties, no promises, no returns, and no responsibility for anything once the deal is concluded. It is caveat emptor (and caveat vendor). You live with what you bought, or without it, as the case may be.

### Nonverbal behavior

About 55% of a negotiator's message is perceived nonverbally; only 7% depends on what is said and 38% on how it is said.

It is not that a single gesture reveals all but how gestures fit in with what we are trying to say. If our gestures contradict our words, then the message received is different from the one sent.

- Crowding the private space of the other negotiator or pumping a stranger's hand as if he were a long-lost friend can destroy the intended effect.

- Touching the face, rubbing the cheek, or covering the mouth can signal that someone is being less than candid; it can also mean that she has an itch or he was eating garlic last night.

- Chin stroking can mean a decision is imminent. It is not sensible to interrupt someone's thoughts at this point.

- If the other negotiator sits back with arms folded and appears about to say something, it is almost certainly going to be "no." At this point, swift intervention to review the positive points in your PROPOSAL may be helpful.

- Arms folded across the chest is a defensive gesture suggesting that the other negotiator does not accept what you have said.

Repeating your point only forces the other person to dig in. Perhaps some QUESTIONS would reveal what is wrong with your message from the listener's point of view.

Nonverbal behavior is underrated by some people and overrated by others. A brilliantly manipulated message is unlikely to be successful if the content is unacceptable, and a badly sent message that is otherwise acceptable could be rejected because the listener has grave doubts about your true intentions.

## Nonzero sum

What you gain is not at my expense (see **zero sum**). The sum of the positive gains is greater than zero.

Suppose you are negotiating such issues as these:

- **PRICE** per unit
- Quantity to be delivered
- When payment is to be made
- Specifications
- Policy on returns of defective units

Your **INTERESTS** as the buyer may be served best by a delayed payment to suit your cash flow, a large quantity in stock to cover surges in demand, and a flexible returns policy to cover for breakage. The seller may be interested in a premium price to move the product up-market, large production runs to reduce unit costs, and specifications that reduce inspection costs.

Trading a higher unit price for delayed payment, trading a different specification for a flexible returns policy, and matching each other's needs for large production and order quantities provide each of you with a nonzero sum settlement. You both make gains without diminishing the gains of the other.

## No problem

A reckless **CONCESSION**.

**Q:** Can you deliver overnight?

**A:** No problem.

**Q:** We need 24-hour call outs on this equipment.

**A:** No problem.

"No problem" concessions are wasted. They might

be prepared to compensate generously, but you do not
know if you do not try.

Put them on the spot:

**Q:** Are you saying that if we do deliver overnight you
will award us the contract?

**Q:** If we can offer a 24-hour service, do we get the
business?

### No sale, no fee

A version of CONTINGENCY PRICING. Payment for services is based exclusively on results.

"No fee" may involve costs (advertising and other
expenses) even when no sale occurs. If a sale takes place
but the fee-earner was not responsible for the sale, does
he or she still get a fee?

People offering "no sale, no fee" contracts may be
building client lists, be desperate for work, or be specu-
lative agents.

### Nothing is agreed

Nothing is agreed until everything is agreed.

Listening to a proposition does not commit you to
agreeing to it (do not interrupt). Asking QUESTIONS about
a proposition does not signify that you agree with it.

Assert regularly that agreement on one issue is not
final and must await consideration of the whole package
(see LINKING).

### Not negotiable

A pressure ploy. Stake out a nonnegotiable area, refuse
to budge, and force the other negotiator to accept your
exclusion of issues from negotiation.

The problem comes if what you are excluding is the central issue that the other negotiator wishes to negotiate about.

Some issues are nonnegotiable, and we prefer to resolve the dispute by other means (war, litigation). But excluding issues does not make them nonnegotiable; if it did, negotiators would narrow the negotiable issues to the ones they felt strongest in or were least concerned about.

### OBJECTION

A defensive move, signaling **INHIBITIONS** about your proposal. Unanswered, objections fuel the inhibitions of the objector.

Do not interrupt well-worn objections with well-worn answers.

❑ Listen to the objection.

❑ Ask **QUESTIONS** for clarification.

❑ Show empathy ("Yes, I see what you are getting at"), not contempt ("Yes, it's true that some less-informed people do worry about that").

❑ Address each objection with a full and frank exposition to eliminate the objector's concerns.

❑ If the objector's worries are founded on a misconception, gently correct it and support the correction with a review of the benefits. Ask positively if all anxieties have been satisfied.

❑ When the objection refers to something your service does not cover, avoid trying to bluff your way around it.

❑ Direct the objector's attention to how the particular concern compares with the benefits of the rest of your proposal.

An objection answered is a step toward agreement.

### OBJECTIVE

Quantifiable objectives are meaningful; nonquantifiable objectives are suspect. If your objectives are vague — "a better deal," "happier employees" — quantify them by considering the steps needed to achieve them.

• What constitutes a better deal?

• What would make the employees happier?

Set a range rather than choose a fixed number. A range gives you negotiating flexibility and forces you to consider alternative **TRADE-OFFS** (your nascent negotiating **STRATEGY**).

The more thoroughly you prepare your objectives across the maximum number of **TRADABLES**, the more confident you will be in negotiation.

### Offer

Can be tentative or specific but should always be conditional: if you do such and such, then I will do so and so.

When making tentative offers, be specific about what other parties must do for you and be vague about what you could do in return.

Being too specific reveals your hand, causing them to revise their **EXPECTATIONS** to your disadvantage. The nonspecific offer is suitable for the **ADD-ON**.

**BARGAINING** offers are always conditional and specific.

If they say "yes" to a specific offer, you have an **AGREEMENT**.

### Offer they must refuse

An **OFFER** deliberately set to be rejected. Contractors overloaded with work **BID** high to avoid winning a contract when not bidding at all would antagonize the buyer and endanger future opportunities.

Tender an offer they must refuse when you wish to avoid any of the following:

- Low-profit contracts
- Contracts below a minimum value
- Places where you do not want to go
- People with whom you prefer not to deal

Introduce unacceptable conditions or demands that are outside the other negotiators' limits, or deliberately declare **NOT NEGOTIABLE** something that is vital to them.

There is one problem: sometimes the offer they must refuse is accepted, and you are left to get on with it.

## OFFSET

Increasingly common and a restriction on free trade. No direct transfer takes place between the supply of goods and the offset activity.

Offsets are largely political counters to lobbying against foreign suppliers.

An offset deal is meant to bring new work to the domestic economy, but it is often merely work that would be placed in the country anyway.

## OFF THE RECORD

One way out of **DEADLOCK** is through an off-the-record discussion. The principals meet for a private discussion, out of earshot of their colleagues, and agree to settle. If using a washroom **ADJOURNMENT**, check the stalls first or else an unseen outraged colleague may put the private talks on the record.

Use off-the-record moves only with negotiators you know well and **TRUST**.

### ONE OFFER ONLY

Procedure whereby suppliers get one chance to offer their best PRICE in competition with others.

One offer only is best used for the regular purchase of standard products that are well specified. It can also be used occasionally for expensive mandatory services (audits, banking and legal services, pension fund management, insurance, and so on). Test the market by calling for tenders for your business for fixed periods of, say, two to three years.

If the specification is unambiguous, there is nothing but price to negotiate. If there is no collusion between sellers, you can be sure of a competitive price (somebody is almost always willing to DISCOUNT a price for business). If the specification is complex, or if the purchase is so separated in time as to be unusual, purchase by negotiation. Not being too sure about what you want could lead you to specify something that negotiation could improve on.

### ONE PRICE, ONE PACKAGE

A seller's defensive ploy. You can expect the other negotiators to push you either on the PRICE or on the package, or both. To clinch the deal, they "need" this or that extra, or demand them as add-ons inclusive of your quoted price (see YES, BUT).

❐ Apply the principle "this package, this price; that package, that price."

❐ Flush out all the extras or changes to your proposed package that the buyer wants. This blocks off a "yes, but" approach.

❐ Price the extras or changes as another package.

❐ TRADE changes in the package against the change in the price.

Failing to price package changes undermines their value (free gifts are seldom appreciated), and you miss an opportunity to show the buyer that you negotiate by trading not by conceding unilaterally.

Precedents are promises for the future.

### ONE-TRUCK CONTRACTS

A risky way to do business. You undertake a transaction with a minimum of discussion about the contingencies that might arise. If these contingencies are expensive, there is a RISK of a liability claim.

Hiring a truck with a minimum of fuss has its advantages: "One truck, $150-a-day rental." But the truck will be used for some purpose, which raises all kinds of questions.

- Who pays for repairs while the truck is on hire?
- Who recovers the vehicle if it breaks down?
- Who pays for fuel?
- Will it be replaced if it is stolen or breaks down?
- Who is legally liable for its mechanical condition?
- Is it warranted for the use to which it will be put?

Profitable rental companies use preprinted contracts that cover every imaginable contingency either in detail or through a LIFEBOAT CLAUSE, which may be why they are profitable. Consider all the possible contingencies in your deals and negotiate for them to be covered.

### ON TAKING IT PERSONALLY

Negotiators are human: they get upset. Occasionally even seasoned negotiators get extremely angry, make threats, raise their voices, shout, curse, and remonstrate. Sometimes they walk out to protest the other negotiator's behavior.

Most negotiators slip into unprofessional involvement some of the time. In negotiating, do not take it personally or we will all be worse off.

### OPTION

When buying, offer the seller an option instead of a deposit; this "locks in" the seller to the transaction.

Offer a cash consideration for the purchase of a legally binding option to buy the property by a given date for an agreed-on PRICE. If for any reason you fail to buy the property, the seller keeps your option money. When you exercise your option to buy, set the option money against the purchase price.

Will a seller accept an option-to-purchase AGREE-MENT? That depends on the terms of the option.

Options can also refer to the development of possible solutions to a problem in a noncommittal way so as to tap into the parties' creativity rather than their conflicts. Production of options is the hoped-for product of BRAINSTORMING.

### ORDER TAKING

A sign of a jaded sales force. Sellers who merely meet customers to take their regular orders are missing opportunities to negotiate better orders. It might be cheaper for a company selling from a regular low-value list to use a marketing operation.

### OR ELSE

An ultimatum ploy: "Either you meet our demands, or else we call a strike."

Such ploys can provoke the very resistance they are meant to overcome. If the other side believes that your THREAT is empty or can be ridden out, it might choose to take the "or else" consequences rather than give in. The other side might be defiant enough to take the "or else" option even though you have overwhelming POWER.

### OVER-AND-UNDER PLOY

The impossible response to the impossible demand. The other negotiator sometimes springs an impossible demand on you: "Give me 5% for a three-day settlement discount."

Spring back an over-and-under: "If you agree to a 5% premium for late payment."

### Packaging

Putting elements of various proposals into a package to make them mutually acceptable. By repackaging the mutually contradictory or overlapping parts of competing proposals you move toward **BARGAINING**.

Packages address the **INTERESTS** and **INHIBITIONS** of each party. If the other side is keen on the money (interest) but worried about getting paid (inhibition), repackage your **PROPOSAL** to meet these requirements without jeopardizing your own.

- Can you repackage in a different way?
- What are the shared interests in particular options?
- Can you **TRADE** movement on one **OPTION** for movement on a less important one?
- What might you want for offering the other side what it wants?

### Padding

A negotiating margin. The padded **PRICE** gives sellers negotiating room. When the buyer expects some movement and you have no room to move, you could end up losing the business or buying it at the expense of your profit.

Pad prices when

- you anticipate last-minute demands;
- the other party does not have final **AUTHORITY**;
- you expect a competitive rebid ploy;
- dealing with price-blind clients;
- you can avoid a **COST BREAKDOWN**;

- you have to wait for your money;
- a **COUNTERTRADE** proposition is likely;
- you can get away with it.

### PARTNER

A partner shares your problems and the profits. Disputes between partners originate from differing perceptions of how each fits into the future direction of the business. Partnerships that break up are more complicated than a divorce so it is better to negotiate terms before the partnership is formed than when a breakup is imminent:

- Negotiate an agreement on how the assets and liabilities will be shared in the event of a dissolution or divorce.
- Negotiate the rules for removing from the partnership somebody who is incompetent or otherwise no longer suitable.

You feel the need for a partner most when you need access to capital or contacts. But why give away things you will value later for things you value now, if the consequence is that you have to share everything (the worth of the business, plus its profits) long after your initial needs have been met. Can you offer a high return on the capital invested rather than a partnership? Once you pay the lender off, everything you created remains yours.

### PARTNERING

Different parties become partners in trying to reach a common objective. Thus in a construction project, for example, the owner, the builder, the subcontractors, and sometimes the unions become partners in the project.

Partnering requires drawing up a set of rules for relating to one another as the project goes along, with mechanisms for negotiations and mediation at various stages so that disputes are resolved as soon as possible, rather than allowed to fester and create ill will among the parties. Partnering is now common in the construction industry worldwide.

### PATENTS AND LICENSES

Products and services can be licensed. The licenser receives income for creating a product or service that the licensee exploits in a defined territory.

Consider the following when negotiating licenses:

- ❏ What is the licenser granting to the licensee and for which territory?
- ❏ What is the licensee entitled to market or sell?
- ❏ Which specific patents, trademarks, and know-how is the licenser licensing?
- ❏ How exclusive is the license?
- ❏ Is the licensee allowed to sell outside the territory?
- ❏ Independently of the licensee, can the licenser also supply the licensee's territory?
- ❏ Are other licensees of the licenser permitted to sell or supply in the licensee's territory?
- ❏ If the licensee fails to meet market targets or to supply known demands for the licenser's products or services, can the licenser supply direct or contract with another licensee to do the same?
- ❏ How much and when does the licensee pay for the license?
- ❏ Is the license fee a royalty on gross or net turnover?

❒ If net, how is this defined?

❒ How regular are the payments to be?

❒ What separate accounts should the licensee keep? How regularly may they be inspected? Who shall audit them?

❒ How long should the AGREEMENT last?

❒ What notice is required to terminate the agreement?

❒ Under what conditions can premature termination occur (breach of contract, FORCE MAJEURE, bankruptcy of licensee, merger or takeover by another company)?

❒ What must the licensee undertake when the license is revoked for any reason? What restrictions on the licensee are imposed? What happens to all current stocks or client services?

❒ What obligations does the licensee have to preserve confidentiality both in and out of contract?

❒ What guarantee of quality must the licensee give regarding the production or supply of the licenser's goods and services?

❒ What restrictions are to be imposed on the licensee for supplying similar goods or services?

❒ What training and support is the licenser to supply to the licensee, and who pays for them?

❒ How are disputes between the licenser and the licensee to be resolved and which country's law applies?

## PATIENCE

More than a virtue, patience is imperative. TIME is the most expensive cost of negotiating. Patience reduces time pressures.

- If the negotiation is likely to be a long one, arrange coverage of senior staff so that other work does not suffer.
- Rotate staff to reduce isolation and fatigue.
- Reduce your reliance on the outcome of the negotiation by competing for other work.
- If you desperately need the business from a long-haul negotiation, consider your BATNA.
- Sit it out, but send patient people to negotiate.
- Whoever has the least patience concedes faster.

### PENALTY CLAUSE

Assurance against failure to comply with promises. The penalty can be a fixed or escalating sum.

When pressing for penalty clauses, assert that if the other negotiators have confidence in their performance, they have no reason to fear them.

Resist penalties if the nature of the work creates unique uncertainties such as the following:

- Unforeseeable geological conditions
- Narrow weather windows
- Special safety hazards
- Political instabilities that threaten access and egress
- Legal complications
- Dependence on suppliers outside your control
- Technological frontiers
- Untested designs
- Reliance on client's data
- Subjection to client's changeable specifications and managerial directions

Your performance guarantees operate only if the following conditions exist:

• Spares, inputs, and materials meet your own specifications.

• Everyone connected with the process is trained to your standards.

• The working environment is suitable for the process.

• You have the right to on-site inspection, to replace or repair, and to decide if any working practice is in violation of your warranties.

Insist that the penalty clock stops if delays are caused by the client's failure to meet obligations; it is restarted (at your confirmation) only when the client complies. This moves not just the dates of the immediately affected segment, but all consequential critical dates to new later dates.

Penalty clauses are sometimes used to beat "unfair trading," dumping, or illegal subsidy rules. The supplier quotes a PRICE with a substantial delivery penalty and ensures that delivery is delayed. The penalties come into force and reduce the price. You get a reputation for poor delivery, but you get the business.

### PENDULUM ARBITRATION

The arbitrator must choose one or the other negotiator's FINAL OFFER and not seek a compromise between them.

A negotiator could be encouraged to refuse to settle because an arbitrator's decision is a compromise between the two final offers and improvement in the other negotiator's final offer is bound to result.

When the arbitrator is using pendulum arbitration, however, the negotiator must ensure that the final offer is not too extreme because the arbitrator is likely to choose the other negotiator's less extreme position. Adjusting the final pre-pendulum arbitration offer to make it attractive to the arbitrator also makes it more attractive to the other negotiator. When both negotiators do this, they become more conciliatory, which improves their chances of finding a solution.

### Perception

Seeing ourselves as nobody else does.

Other people's behavior influences your perceptions, and what you perceive confirms or amends your ASPIRATIONS. Other negotiators attempt to influence your perceptions in order to

- restructure them in their favor;
- shake your faith in the viability of your current offer;
- increase the sense of inevitability of settling at their current offer.

You structure your opponent's perceptions by your apparent

- willingness to DEADLOCK;
- indifference to settling quickly;
- confidence that you have options;
- resolve not to compromise;
- professional success;
- confidence in your current PROPOSAL;
- willingness to listen;
- reasonableness.

Use the following ploys:

❏ Weaken your opponents' confidence. Ask for the criteria, method of calculation, statement of the facts, and references to precedent or convention that support their case; then look for inconsistencies, alternative facts, dubious ASSUMPTIONS, omissions, and unwarranted conclusions.

❏ Deter resort to COERCION. Assert your desire for a negotiated settlement to save avoidable costs to both sides. Adjourn to "cool off" and think through the consequences of not coming to an AGREEMENT. Show willingness to continue negotiations for "as long as it takes."

❏ Enhance the viability of your own proposals. Show confidence in your presentation, your grasp of detail, your willingness to understand their needs and to consider options that bridge your differences, and your intention of coming to an agreement as soon as possible (although you are more than willing to wait, if need be).

## PERFORMANCE BOND

Varying degrees of onerous burdens imposed by powerful buyers on desperate sellers. Originally the performance bond protected the client from shoddy work.

A performance bond concentrates your efforts to deliver your promises. If you fail, the buyer cashes the bond and receives compensation.

Some performance bonds are irrevocable and unconditional, allowing buyers the right to cash them as fancy dictates. To agree to such constraints is an act of reckless desperation, irrespective of the quality of your performance. But when refusal to agree to a performance bond disqualifies you on the grounds that you have something to fear, you agree.

Performance bonds shift the RISK from the buyer to the seller (if buying, demand one). The risk is transformed from one of your performance into one of whether the buyer will invoke payment, regardless of your performance. The POWER balance determines whether you agree to their terms.

Unscrupulous officials sometimes press for a bribe as an inducement for them not to present the bond for payment.

## PERRY MASON PLOY

Behaving like legal counsel and interrogating the party you are trying to negotiate an AGREEMENT with.

The Perry Mason ploy consists of asking a string of QUESTIONS, the answers to which are at first apparently innocuous. As they receive the answer "yes," they move in for the "guilty" question.

This ploy is illegitimate. There is no connection between the lead-in questions and the ultimate question. If you answer their questions, they pronounce you "guilty." Hence it is best to answer no questions at all.

*Counter:* Ask, "What exactly are you getting at?"

## PERSONAL RELATIONSHIPS

Never underestimate their value. Only trespass on them once. Do not rely on them. Business is business.

Although you seek to cultivate sound personal relationships based on demonstrated TRUST and reliability, you must realize that other people's commitment to your INTERESTS is fragile when the bullet slides into the breach.

Commercial negotiators, diplomats, and bargaining agents inevitably form relationships, if only through their professional interaction. These relationships are important, however tentative they may be, for negotiating with somebody you do not know is more difficult than negotiating with somebody you know.

The basic principle of establishing a personal negotiating relationship with others is to assist them to achieve their OBJECTIVE within the boundaries of your own. In short: do not take undue advantage of their predicament.

### PERSUASION

The most common form of discourse when you face a problem.

People whose INTERESTS are different from yours are not easily persuaded if the stakes are important to them. When they are not persuaded by your reasonable, logical, and sensible statements, you are frustrated, you become annoyed, you perceive a wickedness in their inability to see your point of view. The result is an ARGUMENT.

You will limit the likelihood of failure if you practice the following:

- Attempt to persuade them of simple, easy-to-agree-on points rather than complex, controversial issues.

- Emphasize your eagerness for reaching an AGREEMENT, not for forcing them to comply (that is, do not mix persuasion with threats).

- Restrict yourself to supporting your position with a

few robust arguments that stand up to scrutiny rather than diluting them with spurious arguments that collapse as soon as the weakest is challenged.

• Appeal to the other party's self-interest rather than recognition of what you deserve.

### POSITIONAL BARGAINING

Building a position for oneself and then fortifying it.

Negotiators can get stuck into defending positions instead of seeking a solution. Defending a position can lead to attacking the other party's position, which leads to destructive **ARGUMENT** and **DEADLOCK.**

Repetitive defenses of positions harden the negotiator's stances and stifle creativity (see **PRINCIPLES 2**). Try to move from positional bargaining to more interest-based bargaining, getting at your underlying concerns rather than merely your surface positions.

### POWER

Like the wind, felt rather than seen. You have power over the other negotiators to the extent that you can induce them to do something they would otherwise not do and vice versa.

Your **BARGAINING** power, as is the other negotiator's, is a function of the relative costs of disagreement to each of you. Specifically:

$$\text{Your bargaining power} = \frac{\text{cost to them of rejecting your terms}}{\text{cost to them of accepting your terms}}.$$

$$\text{Their bargaining power} = \frac{\text{cost to you of rejecting their terms}}{\text{cost to you of accepting their terms}}.$$

In general, if your power ratio is greater than unity (the costs of rejection are larger than the costs of acceptance), then you have bargaining power over the other side.

Operational content can be derived by calculating the actual costs of rejecting the other side's OFFER. These costs must be probabilistic: there is no certainty that the last offer is the FINAL OFFER or that the threatened, or implied, consequence (STRIKE, LOCKOUT, canceled contract, divorce, war, and so on) will materialize. Moreover, your estimates of the costs of accepting the last offer may be pessimistic.

Power is subjective. You perceive the other side's power according to many influences on your mind, some of them unconscious, some mistaken, and some manipulated by the other side itself.

### PRAISING THE PRODUCT

Do not. It only encourages them to charge more for supplying it.

### PREEMPTIVE BID

An attempt to jump a line before an AUCTION. You BID an amount sufficient to induce the owner to accept it in preference to waiting for the auction. If the bid is high enough, the inducement is plain.

To apply extra pressure, try the following:

- Make your preemptive bid conditional on its almost immediate acceptance.
- State that if the bid is rejected you will not rebid subsequently at any PRICE whatsoever. Mean it.

### Premium pricing

Premium products are marketed at higher prices than others. The price markup may not reflect anything substantial in terms of product differences. If the other negotiators perceive your product to be superior to substitutes, they may be persuaded to pay a premium price.

### Preparation

Jewel in the crown of effective negotiation. Get this right and your performance in the negotiation dramatically improves.

The best preparation is knowing your business better than anybody else. If you do not know your business well enough, you can rely on your rivals to teach you. Ask yourself the following questions:

❑ What are my INTERESTS?

❑ What are the issues? Itemize the details for negotiation.

❑ What do I want for each issue?

❑ How important is each want to me? Prioritize:

> *high importance* (must get or definitely no deal)
>
> *medium importance* (intend to get or perhaps no deal)
>
> *low importance* (like to get but will still deal)

❑ What are my entry offers? Quantify them.

❑ What are my exit offers?

❑ What do I *not* want, and how badly? (See INHIBITIONS)

❑ What might the other negotiators want?

❑ What might be their entry offers?

❑ How might they prioritize their wants?

◻ What information do I have that helps me?

◻ What information could hinder me if disclosed?

◻ What information do I need to verify my ASSUMP-
TIONS?

◻ What is my STRATEGY? Keep it simple.

◻ What happens if it is not working? Select a fallback
strategy.

Write everything down. A preparation planner is a
useful tool for developing your ideas (see the figure on
page 171). List wants in a column down the left-hand
side of the paper.

• Allocate degrees of importance to your wants (high,
medium, low) and put them together in the column.

• Establish a range rather than a fixed number for each
want.

• Write your entry offer for each want on the left and
your exit offer on the right.

### PRICE

First unassailable law of the MARKET: the selling price
of something is not what it cost its owner, but what it
is worth to the person keenest to acquire it.

The total revenue from sales equals price per item
times quantity sold. The total cost from producing the
items equals cost per item times quantity produced. If
total revenue minus total cost is greater than zero, you
make a profit. If it is not, you do not. To stay in business, find enough buyers keen to acquire your output at
a price that raises total revenue above total costs.

The trouble is that your costs are your affair but your
selling price is set by the market.

### Preparation Planner Objectives

| Wants | Importance | Entry Offer | Exit Offer |
|-------|------------|-------------|------------|
|       | High       |             |            |
|       | Medium     |             |            |
|       | Low        |             |            |

All companies' problems boil down to price. To survive profitably, you must drive down costs per unit (search for efficiency) and find the price that captures the most profitable total revenue (net of marketing costs).

Troubles begin when companies kid themselves by doing some version of the following:

• Altering attributions across cost headings
• Changing depreciation practice, and so on
• "Marginal cost pricing"
• Pricing for "contribution to overheads"
• Pricing to "fill unused capacity"
• Pricing to "clear the unsaleable stock"

#### PRICE NEGOTIATION

Prices are determined by the MARKET, but you do not sell to markets, you sell to people, and these people do not have perfect information. Imperfect information is both your edge and your torment.

If buyers are lining up six deep to buy your stock, your PRICE will be higher than if you are in a six-deep line of sellers waiting to sell it. But if it comes down to price alone, consider getting out of that line of business.

A price negotiation is a ZERO-SUM game. Your most profitable strategies include the following:

❐ Widen the negotiation from price to other TRADABLES.

❐ Separate yourself from the competition.

❐ Form a line with only one person in it: yourself.

❐ Go for the big numbers (test the quantity discounts available from sellers; test the total revenue available from buyers).

❐ Go for the add-ons.

❐ Test the buyer's price sensitivity.

❐ Test the seller's markup.

❐ Go for the cooperative relationship.

❐ Test the buyer's INTERESTS.

❐ Test the seller's reliability.

❐ Go for the mutual WIN-WIN.

❐ Test the buyer's room for maneuver.

❐ Test the seller's room for maneuver.

❐ Enter not too close to your exit price.

### PRICE VERSUS COST

A ploy to protect a PRICE from a buyer's challenge. For example:

**Seller:** Do you want low price or low cost?

**Buyer:** I don't follow you.

**Seller:** Low-priced products cost more when you use them. They break down more often and have a short life.

**Buyer:** You just want me to pay your high price.

**Seller:** Sure I want you to pay my price, but I also want you to benefit from a longer-lasting product with lower costs over its longer life than a cheapie.

**Buyer:** So?

**Seller:** Well, you pay my price only once, but how many times will you pay for the cheapie?

### Price war

Avoid it. Move into some other business. Move upmarket or move downmarket or move sideways, but do not join in.

Price wars are won by the big battalions. If your market share is 1%, you will not drive a *Fortune* 500 competitor out of the market by slashing your prices. The competitor could give your 1% volume free to your customers and wait until you ran out of breath.

If you cannot keep out of a price war, the objective is to survive, not to win (for there are no winners).

### Principal

The organ grinder. The advantage of dealing with principals are as follows:

- They make the final decision.
- They can authorize changes.
- They can accept unusual offers.
- They are closest to the money.
- They can come to a decision quickly.

- You have equal status.

The disadvantages of dealing with principals are these:

- There is no appeal against their final decision.
- They are not always on top of the detail.
- They are too busy for slow-moving negotiations.
- They do not believe in equal status.
- They are emotionally involved with their properties.

### PRINCIPLES 1

Sometimes it is necessary to rise above them.

Negotiators who admit to having principles often mean the beliefs that sanctify their prejudices. These people are extremely difficult to negotiate with, for their "principles" are a barrier to movement.

### PRINCIPLES 2

"Never yield to pressure, only to principle" (Roger Fisher and Bill Ury).

General principles that are independent of the negotiators are seen as aids to **AGREEMENT**. Instead of battling over conflicting demands, the negotiators search for objective criteria to judge the merits of alternative solutions.

If objective criteria are agreed on (and this is not certain: see **FORMULA BARGAINING**), they become the principles that determine the joint solution.

You appeal to criteria independent of both of you.

- "Fair standards" or "fairness" generally
- Market evaluation
- Scientific measurement

- Legal precedent
- Actual costs
- Agreed-on objectives
- Equalization of misery/profits/risk

This does not preclude a dispute about the criteria. You may have to modify your demands in the light of the mutually chosen criteria and you must be willing to do so.

If pressure is applied, insist on determining the issue on principles. If they have the POWER, however, it is usually decided their way, not yours. This is the weakness of this principled approach: there is seldom a unique set of objective criteria for each dispute. Indeed, the parties can DEADLOCK over the choice of criteria, with each backing a selection that enhances its own position, taking us back to the problems of POSITIONAL BARGAINING.

### PRIORITIES

Best sorted out in PREPARATION, not while negotiating face to face. Wants are not all weighted with the same degree of priority; otherwise there would be little room for movement. Some issues are more important than others and their ranking should be decided beforehand.

It is in the difference in priorities with which the negotiators approach the issues that the solution is found.

- Anything that the other negotiators value more than you do is open to a TRADE for those things that you value more than they do.
- It is not what it is worth to you that is decisive; it is the relative value to them.

- Your low priorities are not "giveaways"; the other side may value them more than you do.
- Paradoxically, the more other negotiators value particular outcomes, the more POWER they give you if you value those outcomes less than they do.
- Power is balanced when the values of the issues are inversely related.

Events in the negotiation revise your priorities. Establishing your priorities is an organizing, not a stultifying, activity. It ensures a grasp of the detail.

### PRISONER'S DILEMMA

There is no correct solution to a dilemma; that is why it is a dilemma.

You face many dilemmas in negotiating: where to open, when to move, whether to agree or to DEADLOCK. You resolve the dilemma by whatever choice you make but your choice cannot be reversed.

Prisoner's dilemma is a mind game that illustrates the meaning of a dilemma. Two suspects are questioned by a district attorney (DA) who suspects them of having committed a major crime but does not have enough evidence to convict them. The DA does have enough evidence to convict them both of a lesser offense.

The prisoners are interviewed in separate rooms with no possibility of communication. They are each given a choice between confessing and not confessing to the serious crime. The DA's proposition is as follows:

- If you confess, but your partner does not, you turn state's evidence and go free, and your partner gets 20 years.

- If you both confess, you each get 10 years.

- If neither confesses, you each get 5 years for the lesser offense.

If you were a prisoner, what would you do? Your consideration of the options and your hesitation between them is an example of a dilemma.

Dilemmas are relevant to the negotiating situation. They help spell out the implications of the COMPETITIVE STYLE and the COOPERATIVE STYLE of behavior. Going for short-term gains can severely damage your long-term gains. Going for long-term gains (not exploiting your BARGAINING position) could be beneficial in the long run, but it is risky in the short run if you are modifying your gains with someone who regards you as a one-off temporary partner. (See TIT-FOR-TAT)

### PROBLEM SOLVING

Requires TRUST between the parties and confidence in each other's motives. Unilateral attempts to problem solve a dispute expose you to STRATEGIC INTERACTION by the other negotiators if they continue to use a COMPETITIVE STYLE.

Problem solvers aim to do the following:

- Maximize joint gains

- Focus on common INTERESTS, not differences

- Be nonconfrontational and nonjudgmental

- Apply standards of fairness, common sense, and reasonableness (see PRINCIPLES 2)

They believe the other negotiators can be motivated to replace egoism with enlightened self-interest.

## PROCEDURE

Formal negotiating procedures are common in COLLEC-TIVE BARGAINING.

Procedure agreements between a TRADE UNION and an employer set out formal recognition of each side's rights and INTERESTS.

Employees are required to take up any GRIEVANCE with their immediate manager in the first instance. A failure to agree means the next level of management must be contacted, usually through, or accompanied by, an officially recognized shop steward.

If the shop stewards cannot settle the grievance, the local union official will be accorded higher-level access with the company. When the company has more than one plant, the higher-level management will deal with the national officials of the union.

A grievance that survives the early opportunities for resolution is usually of significance to both sides. The union will take a view on the significance of the member's grievance and how it relates to union policy. In theory this filters out trivial grievances. In practice the union removes the filter when it wishes to impose pressure on the company by letting grievances through to use up management time.

Companies negotiating formal procedures with a union should do the following:

❐ Reject so-called closed shops or 100% union-membership agreements.

❐ Require that membership remain a voluntary decision of the employees.

❐ Insist that nonmembers will not be discriminated

against in any respect (they will have a parallel grievance procedure).

❏ Require the **AGREEMENT** to be of fixed, rather than
indefinite, duration.

❏ Include a statement that "no accredited shop steward
will be accorded special privileges as an employee and
at all times will be subject to the normal disciplinary
rules that apply to all employees."

❏ Reserve the right to communicate directly with all
employees on any matter, and at no time concede
this as an exclusive right of the union.

❏ Exercise this right on a regular basis, as communicating with employees only in crises with the union can
be counterproductive.

### PROGRESS PAYMENT

Reduces exposure on long lead-time projects. Paying for
materials for major construction projects imposes costs
on the supplier (the capital tied up has a cost in its alternative profitable uses). There is also a **RISK** of financial
failure by the client, of a change of government policy
or a change of government, or of a cash crisis in your
own operation.

Progress payments are made for identifiable progress
on the project. They can be triggered by completion of
specific stages, from the arrival of the materials for pro-
cessing through to delivery on site and fabrication.

Alternative systems include these:

• Paying up to one-third of the cost on signing the contract.

• Paying one-third at specified stages during the
project.

- Paying one-third (less 5%) on completion.
- Retaining a 5% balance as security against unforeseen or hidden failings in the structure and an unwillingness on the supplier's part to rectify the problem.

Demand interest on the retained balance.

### Promise

Best kept.

### Proposal

The only thing that can be negotiated. You cannot negotiate an ARGUMENT, a belief, an opinion, a prejudice, a principle, a hope, a GRIEVANCE, a fancy, or a fact.

- A proposal is a tentative solution.
- A bargain is a specific conditional OFFER to settle.
- Proposals are best made putting the condition first: if you will do the following, I am prepared to consider doing such and such.
- If the other side does not accept your conditions, it cannot have the benefits of your offer.

Proposing discloses information about your settlement range, it being impossible to propose and simultaneously hide your offer. That is why your proposal is specific about what you want them to do and vague about what you would do in return. The vagueness ("consider," "look at," and so on) loosens your commitment to a specific number or a course of action.

By statute, custom, necessity, convenience, or tactical advantage, some negotiations require that initial proposals be made in writing. These should follow an entry offer format.

- Pad the offer if it is open to informal negotiation (answering a request for broad details of charges).
- Pad the offer less if it is open to formal negotiation (approaching an imminent decision or two offers only).
- Propose close to an exit offer if it is a competitive **BID** (**ONE OFFER ONLY**).

Verbal proposals have the advantage in that you avoid the necessity of revealing your entry point before you have assessed the other side's **EXPECTATIONS** through constructive debate. The disadvantage of verbal proposals is that you can fumble the presentation, disclose too much about your **PRIORITIES** and true **ASPIRATIONS** (see **NONVERBAL BEHAVIOR**), and make premature **CONCESSION** exchanges. To obviate these disadvantages, proposals should be

- stated briefly,
- without long explanations, and
- summarized.

Avoid an instant response to a proposal (written or verbal). Seek

- clarification and understanding,
- details of criteria used, and
- the thinking behind suggestions.

Do

- listen to the answers;
- treat each item neutrally;
- summarize your understanding;
- look for bridges between your respective positions;
- consider possibilities for **PACKAGING**.

## PSYCHOLOGY OF NEGOTIATION

Two great drives of human endeavor are our motivations and our cognitive perceptions. These do not always match.

Motivations are best summed up by a hierarchy of needs, arranged in an ascending order of importance as each level of need is satisfied.

1. Physiological (hunger, thirst)
2. Safety and security
3. Love and belonging (acceptance)
4. Self-esteem
5. Self-actualization
6. Knowledge and understanding
7. Aesthetic

Experimental and empirical evidence for the higher levels of needs, particularly is mixed. But as a working hypothesis it appears to fit most of the facts.

**Physiological.** The starving are hardly likely to be concerned about status (unless it is related to access to food), but satisfying the basic and other needs comes into play. For negotiators these needs are important.

**Safety and security.** A buyer in a new market chooses products that meet his or her security needs (well-known brands, not new ones that might be risky). This is why positioning your product as safe and secure pays off with new buyers entering the market.

**Love and belonging.** Negotiators with a need to be loved (or respected) are vulnerable. They behave according to what they think is pleasing to the people they are dealing with. They try to please everyone. They are no pleasure to deal with. Either experience improves their performance or they quit the business.

**Self-esteem.** Self-esteem, such as the belief that we are worthy because of our professionalism, is a powerful motivator. In negotiating a good deal for our side, or by making the other side work hard for their gains, we become proud of our achievements, especially when set against recognized perceptions of the difficulties involved in achieving what we did. Self-esteem gives us confidence when we negotiate.

**Self-actualization.** This comes from demonstrably achieving first-class results in a negotiation that stretched us to the limits of our powers. The appeal of a search for excellence finds a response among managers driven by this motivator.

**Knowledge and understanding.** Our cognitive perceptions of the world — the beliefs that we work by — have roots that go deep into our psychology, our past, the past of the country we grew up in, and our perceptions of the world as adults.

International negotiations are particularly difficult as the cognitive structures of the collective entity known as the nation are not easily or quickly changed. This explains why critics of their country's negotiating stances on certain international issues (critics who have neither sought nor been elected to public office thus have never had to compromise with the public's cognition of those issues) can often see rational "solutions" to the problems and are perplexed at the failure of the government to adopt them. However, the so-called rational solutions are impractical in the sense that no one articulating them could get elected.

**Aesthetic.** Our cognitive disposition includes our prejudices, folk myths, and taboos. Negotiating with union representatives often means negotiating with people imbued with a sense of the (sometimes mythical) history of their union.

Even when negotiators speak a common language, they often assign totally different meanings to words and expressions.

- "Profit" to a manager may mean "exploitation" and "theft" to a union member.
- "Efficiency" could be perceived as "slave driving."
- A "good deal" to one negotiator can mean a "rip-off" to another.

Internationally, the paucity of common meanings separates the negotiators of more than one country and political system: consider the different interpretations of the words *democracy, justice, rights, welfare, equality,* and *defense* embraced by member states of the United Nations.

There is always a temptation to find contradictions in the cognitive disposition of other negotiators. People are capable of holding passionately to totally contradictory beliefs and to voicing beliefs that are contradicted by their actions. These intrude into the negotiation as naturally as people blow their noses.

- Attacking someone's belief system is never successful.
- If a negotiated peace requires the other side to suspend its entire belief system as a first step, there is little hope of success.

Find ways to advance your proposals without

- setting off psychological resistance;
- antagonizing or threatening the other negotiator's belief systems;
- undermining their personal motivations.

Instead,

- recognize the legitimacy of the other negotiators' personal motivations;
- refrain from disrespect toward their belief systems (no matter how weird you consider their beliefs to be).

Negotiators who are furthest apart in their cognitive perceptions often have strong mutual respect, and this appears to be conducive to reaching a settlement on the practical issues of their relationship when circumstances dictate that such a negotiation is necessary.

### PUBLIC STANCE

A **COMMITMENT PLOY**. By taking a public stance, a negotiator signals commitment to the declared outcome, ostensibly putting pressure on the other negotiators. It sometimes works. The other negotiators know that you cannot back off from a public statement without considerable loss of face. This induces them to believe that you intend to fight tooth and nail for your publicly declared **OBJECTIVE**. Consequently, they give more than they intended.

Alternatively, your public stance imprisons your negotiating flexibility. A reasonable compromise is excluded because it threatens your public credibility.

Journalists are not given to explanations in public interest stories: either you won or you gave in. Your heroic "statesmanship," your finesse, your brilliantly executed maneuver all are lost in the newspaper headline ("Big Mouth Gives In").

Public stances complicate already complicated disputes. Neither side can move because it has publicly declared that it would not do so. AGREEMENT is inhibited by public stances. Think carefully before going public on a negotiating objective, especially in response to the other negotiator's public statements.

## QUESTIONS

Important advice to all negotiators: ask questions and listen to the answers.

Open questions are better than closed ones. Examples of open questions:

- How did you calculate the rental charge?
- What should I do about office security?
- What suggestions do you have for settling this compensation claim?

Open questions invite the listener to respond with extended statements rather than with yes-or-no answers.

Examples of closed questions:

- Do you think this policy is fair?
- Are you in favor of an options clause?
- Can you redraw this boundary?

Closed questions are the most common questions, yet they are the least effective in securing information. There is not a lot you can do with a yes-or-no answer. The room for signaling is restricted, and even if the answer is clear — they say, "No, we do not want it!" — you are not told anything about whether some adjustments in the PROPOSAL would satisfy them.

To unblock DEADLOCK, ask open questions. Consider the type of question you are about to ask. You want to get the most detailed and helpful answers that you can, so ask the right questions (content), the right way (open, not closed).

Avoid questions that

- expose you to mockery;
- expose your ignorance;
- are sarcastic in tone;
- are embarrassing;
- cause trouble;
- are point scoring.

### QUESTION THE CRITERIA

Ploy to undermine the other negotiators' **PROPOSAL**. Proposals based on facts, rules, formulas, **ASSUMPTIONS**, precedents, and interpretations of "fairness" are vulnerable to how they have been formulated.

- Ask them to explain how they arrived at their proposal.
- What data did they use to calculate their figures?
- What statement of principle formed the basis of their claim?

  Watch out for references to the following:

- "Normal" assessments
- "Standard practice"
- "Straightforward" yields
- "Present values"
- "Common knowledge"

  These could hide phony assumptions not applicable in your case.

  Compelling the other negotiators to justify their proposal and its derivation enables you to

- quibble with their assumptions;
- challenge facts;

- learn something about a market with which you are unfamiliar;
- decide on the relevance of their criteria;
- query the reliability of their sources;
- check on the accuracy of their arithmetic;
- question the valuation of intangibles.

Exploring criteria creates negotiating opportunities that were hidden in the plausibility of jargon or assumed expertise.

If you disagree with the criteria the other negotiators have used, you have a more defensible negotiating position than you do if you accept the criteria but disagree with the conclusions.

### Quick deal

Often regretted.

### Quivering quill

A buyer's pressure ploy. Negotiators close to an **AGREEMENT** experience euphoria. The seller is feeling pleased at the prospect of earning the value of the deal, perhaps with some of it as a **COMMISSION**.

The buyer's pen hovers over the contract. The seller's anxieties leap upward: "What do you mean you need another 2% off the price?"

The buyer puts the pen down and sits back. Panic in the seller: "Look, if I give you 1%, will you sign now?"

The buyer picks up the pen and leans over the contract. The quivering quill, having quivered, quivers on: "Make it 1.5% and we have a deal?" Desperation in the seller: "Okay, okay, just sign it."

*Counter:* Same as for **YES, BUT**. Control your euphoria until the deal is signed (see **PATIENCE**).

## RAPPORT

Helpful, but not sufficient to secure a negotiated **AGREE-MENT**. Lack of rapport inhibits agreement.

You can help establish rapport by

- matching your pace to the other negotiators' (particularly across cultures);
- taking a genuine interest in their contribution;
- steering gently toward the settlement you are looking for.

### REALISTIC OFFER

An offer that can be defended credibly, not one that is fanciful. An offer's credibility is decided by the other negotiator.

- If the other negotiator believes your offer is realistic, then it is realistic.
- Unrealistic offers cause dissent, and the other negotiator could break off.
- The further apart you are, the longer it will take to negotiate a solution.
- The other negotiator may be shocked by your offer but might accept your explanation and adjust his or her own **EXPECTATIONS**.

### REGULATORY NEGOTIATION (REG NEG)

Increasingly used in the United States by government to attempt to develop a consensus approach to a proposed new regulation. Sometimes called negotiated rule making, regulatory negotiation consists of identifying all of the interests of stakeholders concerned about the proposed regulation, getting representatives of each to sit at the table, and working together to come up with an agreed-on approach and often agreed-on language. This approach can be contrasted with the "traditional" approach of having the government agency draft the proposed regulation, putting it out for comment, responding to the comments, and then promulgating a final version. The traditional approach tends to lead to far more litigation (and delay in implementation) than the reg neg approach.

## Rent

Rentability determines property values. It is what the asset can earn in the MARKET.

If negotiating for the landlord, maximize the net rentable space; if for the tenant, minimize it. The net rentable space is what is usable by the tenant (whether he or she uses it or not). Watch for the following:

- Measurements running from inside the window alcove to the wall, not the skirting board
- Deductions for central heating apparatus by the walls (when letting, fix a wooden shelf over them and count the space back in)
- How columns in the floor area are treated (if leasing, check that the space they occupy is excluded)
- How stairs, landings, and elevators are calculated
- Charges for common toilets
- Anywhere showing evidence of use; for example, cabinets in the common areas

## RENT REVIEW

Rent reviews adjust rents to market conditions.

The PRICE per square unit of rentable space is determined by what someone is willing to pay for it. Be guided by the rents realized in adjacent or similar buildings.

Most rents are for fixed terms that do not coincide with market movements in supply and demand.

The LEASE will include a provision for a rent review at specified dates.

❑ If you are a landlord in a tightening market, impose an upward-only rent review.

❑ If you are a tenant in a slackening market, delete upward-only.

❑ Landlords should inspect the property regularly to check for chargeable use and to spot misuse.

❑ Tenants should require notice of an inspection to remove evidence of use of uncharged-for space.

❑ Tenants should determine the going rates for rentable space.

❑ Tenants should check the earlier measurements of the property in case some structural change has occurred and its rentable implications have been overlooked.

❑ If facing increased rents, tenants should list the defects to TRADE increased rent for repairs.

❑ Landlords can avoid this situation by imposing full repair and insurance (FRI) terms in the lease, preferably on both an external and internal basis.

Landlords face costs in finding new tenants; tenants face costs in finding new premises. These costs are

avoided by negotiating a new **AGREEMENT**, but they are
willingly faced if the terms are onerous.

Changes in circumstances are reasons for holding
rents, hence, keep the landlord's rental brochures on file
and reread them before a review.

## REPUTATION

Lose it and you reduce your opportunities. As your reputation depends on the **PERCEPTION** of other negotiators,
it is easily lost or damaged, sometimes without good
cause. What reputation do you want? And with whom?

Establish a negotiating reputation: "This company
says what it means and means what it says, even if in
the short run it costs more than it is worth."

A reputation, once undermined, is less easily put
right: it takes only one dispute, where the balance of
power is reversed, for a "tough" reputation to crumble.

Interpretation of motives is not an exact science, and
the same action is judged differently by different negotiators. Being untrustworthy or dishonest will damage a
reputation, perhaps beyond repair. Deals bypass you because of your reputation.

## RESISTANCE PRICE

The exit **OFFER** where you prefer "no deal" to a deal on
worse terms.

At what **PRICE** does it become unprofitable to do business? Do not confuse a desirable with an actual bottom
line. You do not know the full facts before you negotiate, and circumstances may suggest your original resistance point is unobtainable, but beware of rationalizing
a surrender under pressure.

Your resistance price may be established arbitrarily by your seniors; beyond this point you get sacked. If it is unrealistic, the time to discuss that is during **PREPARATION** and not in a post mortem. Think through the implications of, and the criteria used to determine, your resistance price.

## RESOLUTION

One name for the settlement agreement. When parties have resolved their differences, the result is incorporated into an **AGREEMENT**. Resolution is the object of most negotiations.

## RESTRICTIVE COVENANT

A buyer's protective device. Buyers of businesses protect themselves from future competition by negotiating a restrictive covenant on ex-owners. The ex-owner is prevented from opening a similar business close to the original business. How close is negotiable.

For small businesses, the restrictive covenant bars them from trading within the locality; for national businesses, the restriction may apply to the entire country, or even the world as a whole (although courts have ruled against this).

- The ex-owner may be barred from trading in that business, or one closely related to it, for a fixed term of years.
- The restriction may be confined only to the current clients of the business but permit the ex-owner to generate new business.
- The scope may be narrowly defined (brewing but not barring distribution of beer) or widely defined (de-

sign, manufacture, distribution, and finance of the product).

Publishers impose highly restrictive covenants that prevent authors from producing similar works for other publishers that "materially affect the sales of the book," even though they seldom agree not to publish similar books by other authors.

- Some restrictive covenants aim to protect proprietary information, particularly that of their research and development personnel.

- Licensers also impose similar conditions on the employees of licensee firms and require the licensee to guarantee protection of the licenser's know-how.

If asked to sign a restrictive covenant, you should have a minimum STRATEGY to limit the extent and scope of the restriction and its duration.

### REVERSION

A useful clause to protect your INTERESTS in case of default or a failure to meet the contractual obligations by the other negotiators.

Insist that failure to meet obligations, or circumstances such as their bankruptcy, trigger reversion to you of all your rights, property, and monies, irrespective of their obligations to others. This is particularly important in a license AGREEMENT. Liquidators take over property as forfeit in a bankruptcy.

- Make sure that your property unambiguously passes back to you.

- Give notice of reversion as soon as you discover failure on the licensee's part to meet the agreed-on obligations.

- Insert in the agreement that your notice of reversion is unconditionally sufficient for reversion to take effect.

## REVIEW

Post-negotiation review of both successful and unsuccessful negotiations is essential to long-term success.

Like **PREPARATION**, the review should be structured. Use the original preparation plan as the basis for evaluating performance.

◻ How does the negotiated outcome compare with your intentions?

◻ How did the process unfold?

◻ What events were unexpected?

◻ Where in the process do you think you did better/ worse than you expected?

◻ What were the main mistakes?

◻ What were the successes?

◻ What was the single most important lesson of the negotiation?

Draw up a list of actions to tranform these lessons into improvements in future performance.

## RISK

Never eliminated, but it can be reduced or priced. Reduce risks as follows:

◻ Seek **COLLATERAL**.

◻ Restrict the other party's discretion.

◻ Seek guarantees.

◻ Require a **PERFORMANCE BOND**.

◻ Insist on a deposit.

❏ Sell or buy foward.

❏ Help the other party count the money.

❏ Help the other party collect it.

❏ Factor your invoices.

❏ Sell or take an **OPTION**.

❏ Insist on regular payments.

❏ Find out what the trouble is and what will put it right.

❏ Spread the risk across more than one basket (if you cannot do this, at least watch the basket).

❏ Calculate income conservatively and cost liberally.

❏ Cut your losses.

❏ Charge more for the risk.

❏ Judge worth by expected value (see **DECISION ANALYSIS**).

### ROYALTIES

Authors get royalties, but few live like royalty. Royalties are a percentage share in the retail price of the work; they ordinarily start at about 10% for hardcover books and 7.5% for paperback and then escalate moderately as sales increase.

Authors should follow these guidelines:

❏ Require that royalties escalate quickly and that the qualifying quantities are reduced.

❏ Watch for the "new edition" ploy, that is, the royalty clock restarts with each new edition. Go for a continuous count.

❏ Challenge publishers' estimates of resetting costs, especially if you have supplied the text on disk.

◻ Never sell your work for a fixed sum; poor royalties are better than none.

## RULES

In negotiation there are none.

What is proper is decided by the negotiators involved, and even they have no right of appeal.

Informal rules have emerged, but they have no status other than what you accord them. For every rule there is an exception, and for every negotiator there is a time and circumstance where the rule is abandoned.

Some so-called rules of thumb might include these:

◻ Agreements should be honored.

◻ Sanctions are permissible as complements to the negotiation but not as substitutes.

◻ Solutions should not be imposed on a take-it-or-leave-it basis.

◻ Neither negotiator should interfere in the internal affairs of the other to disrupt their negotiating position or cohesion.

◻ Negotiators should act in "good faith" (*ex bona fide negotiari*) and not behave in a reprehensible and destructive manner.

All these rules, and many others, are breachable. Often one negotiator abides by one interpretation of a rule and the other by another.

◻ The alleged "dishonoring" of an **AGREEMENT** is the subject of many renegotiations.

◻ At what point a sanction is unacceptable as a negotiating ploy is hotly contested by negotiators.

❏ Sometimes "take it or leave it" is all that is left when negotiators are faced with obstinacy.

❏ Negotiators interfere in each other's affairs — that is what propaganda, public stances, leaks, rumors, and threats are all about — to weaken the opposing coalition.

❏ Courts and arbitration sittings are full of disputes about "good faith."

### RUSSIAN FRONT

A ploy to make you accept one unpalatable option by forcing you to choose between two unpalatable options, with one of them so unpalatable that you opt for the other.

It is an allusion to the effect on soldiers of threats of being sent to the "Russian front" in World War II. If an officer had the power to send someone to the Russian front, he could exact compliance with his wishes. The soldier would cringe: "No, no, anything but the Russian front." For example:

**Q:** Either you send me a list of the 10 least efficient people to be laid off in your operation, or I will assume that it doesn't matter who is laid off (including yourself) and I will fire 10 people at random.

**A:** Do you want the list typed or can I name them now?

## SANCTION

Any measure aimed to coerce the other party. Sanctions include

**Employee Relations**

- Overtime bans (or bans of any kind)
- Strikes
- Working to rule
- Discriminating against identifiable groups
- Worktime meetings
- Refusing duty
- Withholding necessary consents, documents, and formal requirements
- Occupying places of work to prevent others from working
- Picketing
- Banning specified inputs
- Refusing to work "blacked" materials
- Rigorously applying safety rules
- Mislaying materials, papers, and information
- Sabotage
- Withdrawing special cover (safety, security)
- Sympathetic actions of any kind in support of other disputes
- Clogging up the disputes procedures with spurious cases
- Prolonging meetings to waste time
- Refusing to meet
- Making public statements on confidential matters

## Commercial Relations

- Canceling contracts
- Returning work unfinished
- Holding on to drawings
- Litigation
- Calling in loans
- Changing suppliers
- Withholding consents
- Mislaying necessary documents
- Returning work on trivial technical grounds
- Refusing to pay invoices
- Holding up payments on one contract while there is a dispute on another contract
- Refusing to maintain equipment
- Withdrawing supplies except on onerous or cash terms
- Calling a creditors' meeting
- Appointing a receiver
- Reporting alleged offenses to an official agency, professional body, or the general public
- Withdrawing financial support
- Liquidating the business
- Selling shares
- Placing votes in a shareholders' meeting
- Not electing directors; firing employees, including directors

## Trade Relations

- Discriminatory trade practices
- Quotas

- Tariffs and nontariff burdens
- Selective import controls
- Withholding export guarantees
- Restricting or banning investment
- Selective and general trade sanctions
- Dumping
- Using vetoes in international organizations
- Administrative delays
- Embargoes

**International Relations**
- Withholding support in public
- Working behind the scenes to withhold support
- Making public condemnations
- Joining in coalitions to oppose specific INTERESTS
- Blockades
- Using military force at any level, including war
- Taking hostages
- Taking punitive action against specific citizens
- Terrorism

### SECONDARY BOYCOTT

A coercive measure used by unions, presently illegal in the United States and the United Kingdom; for example, sympathy strikes in unrelated businesses to put pressure on an employer.

### SEEKING CLARIFICATION

Proposals are not always clearly stated. Clarification is essential if you are unclear, and bridge building is essential even if you are clear. People like to be treated seriously. Asking clarification QUESTIONS helps build rapport. Examples:

- Could you go over the second clause? I am not sure how you intend it to operate.
- Am I right in thinking that your liability clause would cover us up to two years from installation?

Questions sometimes finesse explanations that provide additional information about their wants and PRIORITIES. They can lead on to criteria questions.

### SELL AND LEASE BACK

A way to raise capital on your assets.

Lenders supply funds against first-class assets such as prime site properties. You receive the capital for other purposes and lease the properties you formerly owned. Sometimes there are tax regimes that are favorable to these deals.

This could be attractive to a takeover bidder that wants to release funds from the acquired company to reduce borrowings without damaging the income-earning capacity of the business. In the short term the target for the takeover pays for you taking it over. The disadvantage is that you lose control of your properties, and can face rising rents at any subsequent RENT REVIEW.

You could place the company's properties into a separate property company, which then borrows against its property and pays off the borrowings out of rents it charges the parent company for use of the properties. The loan is secured against the property company's assets, and cash is released for other purposes. When the mortgages are repaid, the company still owns its properties.

### SELL CHEAP, GET FAMOUS

A buyer's ploy. Anybody new to a business has no track record. Newcomers cannot attract the premiums that go with experience. Buyers exploit this opportunity. The ploy persuades newcomers to accept a lower price for their services.

**Buyer:** How many plants of this type have you designed?

**Newcomer:** This is my first contract.

**Buyer:** How many times have you been consulted about this type of business problem?

**Newcomer:** I did something similar in my MBA course.

Such buyers are softening you up for a low-fee pitch. But they do not just push you down on price, they make it seem like they are doing you a favor:

- Design this plant for the fee I have suggested, and you will establish your reputation and earn big fees on all subsequent work.
- Invest in solving this problem, and you will soon be quoting in the big league.

You sell yourself cheap to recoup the situation in future business. Some people, finding it hard to get started, offer their services free to clients just to get a track record.

*Counter:* With difficulty, if your track record is a blank sheet of paper. If forced to accept a lower opening fee (do not fall for the "get famous" bit), go for a version of the contingency **ADD-ON:**

- If the design is accepted, then you pay me a second fee equal to 30% of the original fee.

- If my solution is adopted, you pay me another $5,000.

### SHAM OFFER

Using an entry OFFER to disguise your TARGET. You open with a sham offer of $400, leaving room to TRADE back to your target price of $380. Your exit price is $360. Opening at your target forces you to trade below it, which mocks your concept of a target.

If they accept your sham offer, apply the ADD-ON.

### SHOCK OPENING

An abrasive pressure ploy.

The other negotiators open with a PRICE that is wildly outside your EXPECTATIONS. You are shocked into stunned surprise. If they follow through with a credible reason for their PROPOSAL, you have to review your expectations.

The key requirement for a shock opening is credibility. The other negotiators, hearing a shock opening, are forced to reconsider the basis of their own position. "Perhaps our price is too high?"

Even if the shock opening moves the other negotiators only part of the way from their expectations toward yours, it has been effective. There is a risk, however, that you are so far away from their expectations that they break off the negotiations.

### SHUT UP

Silence: there is not a lot of it around. Add to what there is by LISTENING more than you talk. Why? Because you know what is in your mind but you do not know what is in theirs. You will not find out by talking.

Shut up immediately after you

- make a **PROPOSAL**;
- summarize;
- ask a question;
- reach an **AGREEMENT**.

Wait until they respond before you speak again.

Shut up when you have nothing to say. You do not have to fill every silence. Let the power of silence put pressure on them.

### SIGNAL

Subtle change in a negotiator's language, indicating a willingness to consider movement.

- What is "impossible" becomes "difficult."
- What was "never done" becomes "not normally done."
- What was "contrary to company policy" becomes "without precedent or prejudice."
- What was "no way" becomes "not under current circumstances."

Without signals, negotiators would have considerable difficulty in moving without giving the impression that they were about to surrender. Everyone signals — most people do not realize that they are doing so — but many negotiators miss signals because they are not **LISTENING**.

Some negotiators punish the signaler: "I see. So you are no longer holding to your ludicrous opening **OFFER?**" This drives them back to **ARGUMENT**, and delays a settlement. Do not punish a signal. Question it for clarification, and encourage the other negotiator to elaborate:

- You say you have a difficulty with my request. Is there any way that I could make it easier for you to meet my needs?

- Under what conditions would your company be willing to make an ex gratia payment in circumstances like mine?

Signals are normally a prelude to a **PROPOSAL**, and no negotiation can get very far without proposals.

### Sizzle

"Do not sell the steak, sell the sizzle." The world's most successful selling technique, developed by Elmer Wheeler who believed that "the heart is closer to the pocketbook than is the brain."

Find the sizzle in a proposition and put that to them. It goes down better than dry facts. It breaks through their **INHIBITIONS**.

In a competitive **MARKET** why should an exporter ship with you rather than anybody else? Give a reason. Do not sell cargo space (all your competitors have space), sell guaranteed delivery.

Why should a bank choose your firm to liquidate a business? Do not sell accountancy knowledge (competing accountants have that too), sell a hassle-free liquidation.

*Counter:* When buying, buy the steak, not the sizzle.

### Skimmer

Someone who gets between you and the deal, and insists on being "taken care of" before the deal progresses much further. In some countries they pop out of the woodwork unexpectedly. They wait until the contractor is chosen and then get between the contractor and the client. That way they get paid off no matter who wins the contract. Their position (perhaps a connection with the ruling family, perhaps a crucial role in the final decision) guarantees their ability to frustrate the deal. You pay up, or get nowhere.

Sometimes you can block skimmers by making a fuss with their boss, though the skimmer could be working for the boss who prefers not to sully his reputation with an open demand for a bribe.

Try **PADDING** the **PRICE** with the skimmer's payoff if the approach is made before you get to price. If the price is set — that is why you got the contract — the skimmer's (large) fee comes out of your profit.

Beware of people who claim to be able to block your deal but who are in fact only charming chancers. Pay them and you cut your profits, and if the real skimmers turn up demanding their share of the cake, you are going to be working for nothing.

### Skimming

A pricing **STRATEGY**. Some people are **PRICE** blind when it comes to new products. They want the very best and expect to pay for it (if you do not go in high, they think your product is a cheapie).

Luxury cars, yachts, electronic gadgets, new products of all kinds are ripe for a price-skimming strategy. The **MARKET** is limited, deliberately so, but it is lucrative until the competition starts up (they see your pricey products and the people with money wanting to buy them).

Skim the "cream" with the high-price strategy; then expand output and lower prices gradually, as you work your way into the next segment of customers who want the product but are more price sensitive than the people at the upscale end.

### Skinner's pigeon

The late Professor B. F. Skinner of Harvard University claimed that human beings could be conditioned into behavior patterns, given the right stimulus and reward system. The professor demonstrated his theory by training a pigeon to pick out the ace of spades from a deck of cards, no matter how they were shuffled.

The lesson here for negotiators is to consider the relative size of the brains of a pigeon and a human negotiator (roughly a pea to a cabbage). If a pigeon can learn to choose the ace of spades, how much cleverer is a human being learning from the behavior of another negotiator?

Negotiators learn to say no if they find they get concessions when they do so; hence do not stimulate their resistance by rewarding it.

### Softness

Soft negotiators are characterized by their willingness to move in large steps from any position they adopt. Their basic fear is that of not securing an **AGREEMENT**. They

- prefer almost any agreement to **DEADLOCK**;
- negotiate with themselves;
- crumble under threats;
- have an extensive repertoire for rationalizing acceptance of any agreement offered;

- tend also to talk too much;
- qualify any (often unconditional) OFFER they make with a SIGNAL of how far they are prepared to move if it is not acceptable.

## SPLIT THE DIFFERENCE

A settlement ploy. Negotiators stuck on two numbers can move to a settlement by "splitting the difference." You offer $80, they offer $40; splitting the difference gives you $60.

It sounds fair and equitable, and sometimes it is. It can also be expensive; perhaps you cannot afford to split the difference.

To avoid its being sprung on you, stick to numbers that do not have an obvious split point. If your offer is $83.50 and theirs is $40, it is not obvious what number splits the difference, and a number that is not obvious is not so FAIR as one that is.

An offer to split the difference is risky because you disclose a willingness to move 50% of the difference between you. The other negotiators could exploit your SIGNAL and refuse to move, leaving you with a more difficult task in defense of your original number. They could also offer a different split: "I cannot go 50-50, but I will consider 30-70."

When an obvious split point emerges — you have proposed 10% and they have replied with 8% — move to bury the obvious split point by offering 9.85% (conditionally).

If the difference is trivial, there are bigger issues at stake and your relationship with the other negotiators justifies it, agree to split the difference as part of a larger package but not in isolation.

## STAKEHOLDERS

Basic interests affected by a proposed action, often by government or a business. A power company may want to put in a new power line, for example. Stakeholders in this instance would include the people and businesses located along the right-of-way, the construction companies (and unions) doing the building, the banks lending the money, and the consumers of the power to be delivered by the new line. In any multiparty negotiation it is important to identify all of the stakeholders and then decide which ones are essential for a negotiated solution to be implemented.

## STANDARD TERMS

Alibi for loading the contract terms against you.

Sellers often print their terms and conditions on the reverse of their official confirmation letters or on the order forms that they expect you to sign. These standard terms always restrict their liabilities and are onerous to you, not to them, which is why they are printed. Read them carefully. If you cannot accept them all, acknowledge the order in writing with a reference that it is accepted subject to your terms (enclosed), or to the exclusion of their specific term (reference number only). They may be so desperate to receive your goods that they waive their own terms. Later they could change their minds, but the terms are unenforceable once waived.

Printed terms are intimidating. They imply that they cannot be changed (which is why they are often printed close together, so that changes are nearly impossible). To avoid signing an official order form with its specific terms, send an order in writing with your terms on it.

Standard terms are negotiable, but only if you take the trouble to query them.

### STRATEGIC INTERACTION

Jargon from GAME THEORY that describes how negotiators manipulate the information they pass to each other.

You do not know what is going on in the heads of the other negotiators. They are less than candid about their predicament because you might exploit this information. They think how you are likely to react to their behavior, knowing that this is a reaction to your behavior — how you think they think you think they think you think . . . . Taken too far, concern with strategic interaction paralyzes the negotiators into infinite regression.

### STRATEGY

Best kept simple. Complicated strategies fail within a few moves because the other negotiators have not read your script; they have a different plan.

The strategy is dependent on the circumstances and the issues in the negotiation. Not mentioning money, for example, might be a strategic objective when the value of what is for sale is not obvious (neither negotiator knows for certain the other negotiator's evaluation). By keeping money in the background until they have ascertained enough information to set the PRICE, the negotiators prevent an early over or under price being established.

Strategy should be flexible: if it is not working, do not persist. It should also be linked to your marketing and pricing plans.

But above all, remember what Robert Burns said about the "best laid plans of mice and men."

## STRESS

Negotiating is a stressful activity. You are

- anxious about the outcome;
- emotional about the other party's behavior;
- unsure of the implications of offers;
- worried about the other side's intentions;
- concerned about not doing as well as you or your peers expect.

Stress cannot be eliminated; it can be reduced. The professional negotiator tries

- not to take things personally;
- to separate the issues from the personalities;
- to concentrate on INTERESTS rather than issues.

Basically, you should slow down the pace (ask more QUESTIONS), relax before and after sessions, and set realistic rather than fanciful targets.

## STRIKE

Withdrawing labor is a legal right of employees.

Strikes aim to influence negotiation. The strike can be a prelude to a negotiated settlement or a substitute for one. Strikes over highly contentious issues are bitterly fought.

The STRATEGY of the strikers is to prevent normal business from being conducted. The strategy of the employer is to ensure that normal, or near normal, business continues.

If the strikers succeed in stopping normal business,

it is a matter of attrition: Which side runs out of resources first? If the company succeeds in doing its normal business, it is a matter of TIME pressure: How long
before the strikers give up?

Public relations are important in strikes.

- Denouncing strikers as "extremists" when they man-
ifestly are not is counterproductive.

- People who strike before exhausting the opportunities for negotiation are in a weaker position than
those who are driven to strike by the intransigence
of management.

- Avoid being provoked into a strike; you might not be
as indispensable as you think.

- Companies that make public statements about damage done by, or the costs of, the strike strengthen the
strikers (they feel are achieving something).

- Strikes that appear likely to last a long time are over
more quickly than those that appear to be short term.
Hence, if asked how long you can take the strike,
answer, "Indefinitely."

Handling the so-called peace talks is difficult. Public
stances and reports of what is happening are unhelpful.

- If talks fail, avoid shrill denunciations of the other
negotiators: calm acceptance of failure, in sorrow not
anger, wins more votes in the public relations war. It
also makes it easier for talks to recommence when
negotiators are willing to have another go.

- If the strike is a substitute for negotiation, employers
should open the plants to employees who want to
work.

- If you cooperate in closing down your operation with

the strikers, you will enhance the authority of the strike leaders over your employees, which is contrary to your INTERESTS.

### "SUBJECT TO BOARD APPROVAL"

You have been negotiating with the monkeys, not the organ grinders. There is always an organ grinder on the board who thinks he or she could do better than the monkeys and demonstrates this superiority by sending the AGREEMENT back with his or her amendments.

*Counter:* Pad offers that are subject to board approval.

### SUMMARIZING

Simple but effective negotiating behavior.

Negotiations are chaotic. The verbal interaction wanders. People join the flow of conversation and set it off at a tangent (or back to something already covered). Interruptions, both planned and unplanned, occur. A summary refocuses attention on the issues.

* What each side is proposing
* What the differences are
* What has been said about them
* What has been agreed on
* What remains to be agreed on.

Summaries should be short (it is a summary, not a blow-by-blow account) and neutral (cover each side's point of view and what has been proposed).

A biased summary can start an ARGUMENT. A neutral summary placed in the middle of a long bout of verbiage, or at the moment when the debate is wandering off into unhelpful territory, can work wonders on even the most jaded or hot-tempered of negotiators.

Summarize during all phases of the negotiation, particularly

- when argument is dominating the exchanges;
- immediately after your **PROPOSAL**;
- when calling for agreement;
- after agreement has been reached, to check that what you think you have agreed to corresponds to what they believe has been agreed on.

### SWITCH SELLING

Sometimes called bait and switch.

A seller's **ADD-ON** tactic. You think you are negotiating to buy a deluxe model widget, but you find yourself with the super deluxe model. The seller has "switch sold" you up the range.

Sometimes this is to your benefit — the super deluxe model is really better suited to your needs — but often it is not. They advertise a fantastic bargain. When you get there, they have sold out of it, but they do have a few "slightly more expensive" versions available.

*Counter:* Insist on the original deal or no deal.

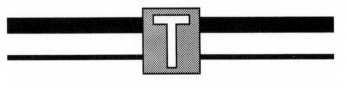

## TABLE

Like the VENUE, if it matters to one of you, it matters to both of you. Negotiators like to sit behind a table, and not only to lay their papers or elbows on it. It is partly instinctive: a table "protects" you in the same way you use your legs and arms to cover parts of your body when you feel threatened or unsure (see NONVERBAL BEHAVIOR).

Negotiators begin in conflict (your solution or mine) and end in cooperation (a jointly agreed-on solution). Putting something between you and them reassures your subconscious anxieties. If you did not feel comfortable, you would perform less well, even display overt antagonism. Some experts, confusing cause for consequence, think negotiators should be forced to sit next to each other in an "open" formation because they believe that tables exacerbate conflict.

## TACIT BARGAINING

Where communication is not possible, or is extremely circumscribed, and the parties make their moves either on how they expect the other party to behave or in reaction to how they perceive them to be behaving (see PRISONER'S DILEMMA).

In competition with a rival firm, you have the choice of increasing your PRICE or maintaining it (perhaps costs are rising and squeezing profits for both of you). As collusion between suppliers is illegal, you face ruinous price competition, but through tacit bargaining you "agree' to raise prices knowing your rival will follow and not exploit your move, so that you both profit.

### TAKE-OFF

Reverse of the ADD-ON. A ploy to raise your PRICE safely, or when a buyer challenges your price and you have padded it.

You quote a price that covers your costs plus add-ons.

**Seller:** My normal price for this service is $700.

**Buyer:** That is far too high, and way outside our budget.

Take off a little.

**Seller:** You realize I have included my travel expenses in the price.

**Buyer:** A bit better, but still . . .

Take off some more.

**Seller:** plus my hotel expenses.

**Buyer:** I see.

You have entered the settlement range.

The take-off enables you to raise your price safely. If challenged, you can retreat a little. If unchallenged, apply the add-on: add your expenses on top of the $700.

### TARGET

The negotiating OBJECTIVE you aim to reach if you can. It is what you want to settle on.

If you open at your target, you are likely to be forced to move away from it, unless they accept your FIRST OFFER.

### TAXATION

An avoidable, but not evadable cost. If tax collectors believe that

• you owe them money in a clear-cut case,

- legal precedent and legislation are beyond doubt, and
- you can pay it,

they issue an instruction to pay and you pay up, subject to your right of appeal. You can arrange payment terms with their consent, but you cannot demand them if you have

- been caught evading payment,
- obstructed their investigations, or
- prevaricated and used outright deceit.

You probably face a prison sentence too.

The tax collector's interest is in collecting as much taxation as the law prescribes (personal promotion and salaries depend on it). Thus, where the legal issues are complicated (no one has devised an unambiguous tax system yet) and the outcome of an appeal to the courts is uncertain, the tax authorities are usually willing to negotiate how much you pay and when you pay it, in order to collect something for certain as opposed to an uncertain amount later, and to avoid the RISK of losing the case and letting others know of the loophole you found (tax cases are widely publicized).

### TEAMWORK

It has advantages and disadvantages. Both can be optimized by PREPARATION and discipline.

The leader carries the bulk of the burden of conducting the negotiation and must make the tactical decisions and call the shots. People not directly involved can slip into the role of spectators, which, as any player will tell you, leads them to assume they can do better. They are tempted into interventions, not always well timed and, in the extreme, they attempt *coups d'état*.

❐ Teams must be disciplined. The only appropriate time and place for criticism and dissent is in a private ADJOURNMENT, not in front of the other negotiators.

❐ Who should be the leader? It is appropriate for the leader to be the best-qualified person, irrespective of seniority.

❐ What do the other members of the team contribute? If there is no obvious answer, why are they there? A lot of TIME is taken up with negotiation, and people who are not needed should do something more productive.

❐ Forming teams solely to match the other team's numbers is not very sensible. A well-briefed team need not be the same size as the other side's. There is no safety in numbers, only expense.

❐ Someone SUMMARIZING is a great help to the leader. Summaries provide well-needed breaks, reduce tension, refocus the negotiations on the issues, and demonstrate that you are LISTENING to what the other negotiators are saying.

❐ Experts and specialists can be consulted or invited to contribute to the discussions on narrowly defined lines. If technical issues are central to the negotiation, have people present who can contribute sensibly but ensure that they are commercially minded. Once technical people start drifting into technicalities, they can destroy a commercial negotiating position. Interactions between your experts and those on the other side should be restricted.

❐ You often need an observer. It is always easier to analyze a negotiation from the observer's position than it is if you are contributing to what is going on. Adjournments give opportunities for the observer to contribute to the assessment of the state of play and to make recommendations for future actions.

❑ Teams should always prepare together. Unbriefed or partially briefed team members are dangerous allies.

## TERMINATION

Essential clause in a contract. A specified date for the termination of the current contract covers you against a perpetual contract that contains, because circumstances change, onerous consequences.

## TERMS OF AGREEMENT

Device for reaching basic agreement on the broad issues before settling the contractual details. Much used in property negotiations.

## THOUSAND EXCEPTIONS

A ploy to weaken the implementation of a policy.

Attacking a policy head-on is not always fruitful. The momentum behind it is so great that it sweeps all before it. For example, instead of helping introduce a policy by restricting its immediate application, you help undermine a policy by limiting its application.

Any policy is vulnerable when its practical details are considered. A general implementation could be limited by the sheer administrative cost of applying it everywhere at once.

❑ Discover awkward exceptions.

❑ Create exceptions.

❑ List exceptions.

❒ Do not indicate your total opposition to the theme of the policy (which its supporters would latch on to and isolate immediately).

The more committed you appear to be to the policy, the more convincing your "regret" that "unfortunately, for the moment, and with current resources, it would be wiser to confine it to this limited application."

### THREAT

Unlike a promise, something that you prefer not to implement.

Threats are part of the repertoire of COERCION. There are two kinds:

- **Compliance.** Unless you do the following specific things, we will do the following to you.
- **Deterrence.** If you do the following things, we will do the following to you.

The consequences of a compliance threat can be avoided by doing what the threatener requires. Examples include threats to

- strike unless the company pays higher wages;
- attack unless a country withdraws its forces;
- leave unless your partner stops drinking.

The consequences of a deterrence threat can be avoided by refraining from doing what the threatener objects to. Examples include threats to

- use force if you attack them;
- strike if you sack employees;
- leave if your partner starts drinking.

Threats are judged on

- the capability of the threateners to carry out the threat;
- the likelihood of them doing so if thwarted in their other intentions;
- the likely effects if the threats are implemented.

Threats raise the tension of a negotiation. A threat cycle is difficult to stop. People do not like to be threatened because, apart from the disagreeable consequences if the threats are implemented, they do not like to have their choices circumscribed. If they comply/desist, it appears they did so because of the threat, thus encouraging more threats, when they may for other reasons wish to adopt a course of action or inaction that corresponds to the threatener's preferences.

Threats may achieve their aims without being implemented, or they may not be believed and have to be implemented or withdrawn. A threat that achieves its ends without being implemented could be the result of a tactical adjustment by the other negotiators, who are temporarily unable to resist the threat. But as soon as those conditions change, they seek revenge.

- Making specific threats is more convincing than being vague, but it is also more restrictive for the threatener. If the threat is ignored, the threatener has little choice but to implement the threat or lose credibility.
- Private threats are more likely to succeed than public ones. If those threatened resent the public loss of face in succumbing to the threat, they might feel compelled to refuse to budge and force the threat to be implemented.
- Vague threats leave the initiative to the threatener as to whether, or how, the threats are implemented, but

the more vague they are, the less convincing they become.

- Bluffing threats are risky because they might be called (loss of credibility). If you must bluff, be vague, as this leaves room for doubt about what triggers the threat's implementation. If those threatened suspect or believe (intelligence, own assessment of the situation) that you are bluffing, they could call your bluff, and you could end up in a war or strike even though you were bluffing originally.

### TIME

The great pressurizer. Negotiations fill the time available, and if that is less than planned for, the negotiator either moves faster more frequently or blows it.

Time pressure

- is uncomfortable;
- adds STRESS to an already stressful situation;
- forces hard choices;
- can split a negotiating team apart, because the members' perceptions of what is now possible do not change at the same rate.

Time can be compressed (we decide by 5 P.M.) or extended (we will call you when we have considered all the proposals). In the former, the negotiators are racing the clock; in the latter, they are watching it.

Negotiators working against time prefer to postpone the other negotiators' making a decision until they have had a full chance to influence that decision. Negotiators kicking their heels waiting for a decision rapidly reach the point where they do not care what decision it is so long as it is a decision.

To minimize the negative effects of time pressure, do the following:

- Have more than one time plan for a negotiation (a long one and a short one) and be ready to work to whichever plan suits the time that becomes available.
- Maintain strong communication links between the negotiators and the home base, including regular briefings if possible.
- Adapt the negotiators to the time context by sending in support if the negotiation is compressed (do not leave it to stressful meetings of pressurized team members), or by pulling out people if they can be used elsewhere while fully supporting those who are left.

### TIT-FOR-TAT

A **WIN-WIN STRATEGY.** Robert Axelrod showed how the best strategy for an indefinite run of dilemma plays is for the players to adopt tit-for-tat. A player cooperates on the first move and from then on does whatever the other player did on the previous move.

The strategy "teaches" the other players that the benefits from cooperation are available if they choose a cooperative **OPTION** (because you always respond positively), but that if they choose to defect, so will you. As the rewards to each from cooperation over the long run are greater than the rewards for defection (defection is always punished), they have a strong incentive to cooperate.

Signaling cooperation without being exploited is the most difficult task facing a negotiator. Tit-for-tat is a workable strategy because it is obvious what you are up to and it is simpler than the alternatives.

It works best when the negotiators take a long-term view of the relationship. Short-term gains can overwhelm intentions to cooperate, although the negotiators know this is irrational in the long run.

When playing tit-for-tat,

- never defect first;
- if the other negotiator defects, react immediately — you have a low threshold to provocation.
- remember that a delayed response weakens your signaled message.

If the others decide to cooperate again,

- forgive them for their defection without rancor;
- immediately respond cooperatively;
- do not exact additional punishment "just to show them." Your OBJECTIVE is to bring them to their senses, not to their knees.

### TOUGHNESS

Much misunderstood. Tough negotiators

- aim for the TARGET, having made proper preparations beforehand;
- are not afraid of DEADLOCK and do not give up easily;
- open with a REALISTIC OFFER and move modestly;
- listen carefully to what the other negotiators say;
- closely scrutinize every detail of what the other party wants;
- move only conditionally (if you . . . then I . . .).

### TRADABLES

The currency of the BARGAINING process. Tradables cover anything, tangible or intangible, over which either party has discretion.

Movement is secured by offering to TRADE something that you have for something they have.

Common tradables include the following:

- Money: PRICE, wages, finance, currency, credit, profits, income, taxes, bonds
- TIME: when it happens, who to, who from
- Goods: quantities, quality, features, substitutes
- Specification: marginal changes, performance standards
- Services: standards, personnel, performance
- Guarantees: guarantor, liability, liquidated damages
- Warranties: duration, extent, coverage
- RISK: extent, who carries it, shares

Considering the tradables available to you as a negotiator gives you ideas for PREPARATION, for new strategies, new proposals, new ways to get out of DEADLOCK.

### TRADE

Never give an inch: trade it. Trading constitutes the singular difference of negotiation compared with other forms of decision making. What is traded may be

- tangible or intangible;
- something in the present or a promise of something in the future;
- of value to both or to only one of the negotiators.

Trade involves exchange. One negotiator gives up something he or she has or controls or can promise for the future in exchange for something the other negotiator has, controls, or can promise.

Negotiation is about the terms of the trade: how much is given in exchange for how much is received.

### TRADE-OFFS

A way to think of the conflicts among values of the people negotiating with each other, leading each party to realize that achieving some results is at the expense of other, often desirable, results. Often people find there are trade-offs in their own positions — for example, that the lower the price they pay, the lower the quality, or that there is a trade-off between PRICE and quality.

Eventually, a settlement may involve some explicit trade-offs: gaining this at the expense of that. But before negotiators assume they are faced with irreconcilable trade-offs, they should engage in as much PROBLEM SOLVING and BRAINSTORMING as possible.

### TRADE UNION

An employee's bargaining AGENT. In theory, most are run by their members; in practice, they are run by small minorities of "active" members. The quality of elections and decision-making processes varies widely. Some members are fiercely loyal to the union, while most blow hot and cold depending on circumstances. It rarely pays to make membership of the union an issue unless it engaged in serious misbehavior (such as intimidation, political strikes).

### TRUST

Earned, not deserved. Trust is unlikely to flourish when the negotiators are

- suspicious of motives, intentions, capabilities, or past behavior;
- hostile for any reason;
- highly competitive;

- contesting vital issues;
- facing big gains or losses;
- feeling threatened;
- ignorant of one another;
- recent victims of trickery.

  Trust does flourish when the negotiators have
- demonstrated their reliability;
- experience of one another in a variety of circumstances;
- invested in confidence-building measures;
- reciprocated in helpful ways and not taken unfair advantage when they could have.

Does trust pay off? Not if its consequences are assumed without being tested. To trust someone recklessly is as risky as dealing with someone who is totally untrustworthy.

If trust is earned by being of proven quality, it pays off handsomely. WIN-WIN outcomes are easier to arrive at if the negotiators are open about their needs without fear of being exploited.

Mutual trust enables the negotiators to increase the size of the pie by exploring, in a safe atmosphere, new solutions to difficult problems.

### UNCONDITIONAL OFFER

Music to the ears of the other negotiators. An unconditional offer is a wasted offer. The other negotiators will accept the offer but come back for more. One-way conceding is no way to conduct a negotiation. Make conditional offers.

### USED-CAR SALE

A classic example of **DISTRIBUTIVE BARGAINING.** Neither you nor the seller knows the other's exit **PRICE**, nor whether the first price mentioned is a **SHAM OFFER** or a **TARGET** price.

Treat a **FIRST OFFER** as an offer that can be improved on. Whatever the seller opens with, no matter how good it looks alongside your target and exit prices, **HAGGLE.** Convince sellers that

- they prefer a sale on terms more favorable to you than they originally expected to get;
- your terms for the car are less favorable to them than they expect;
- a quick certain sale to you now at a lower price than they want is better for them than waiting for another customer;
- you will settle at once if the price is right.

All positive comments on the vehicle's characteristics, or the maker's reputation, or your need for it undermine your stance.

Sellers ask early on what price range you are interested in. They are assessing your exit price, not saving you time looking through their range. So do not tell them. Ask to see their cars. Once sellers have invested time in trying to sell you a car, they are even keener to come to a deal.

❑ Take up their TIME.

❑ Ask QUESTIONS.

❑ Keep them waiting while you go over every inch of the vehicle.

❑ Don't show interest in a particular vehicle.

❑ Let them revise downward their likely profit in order to close the deal.

## VALUING CONCESSIONS

It is not what it is worth to you that counts, but what it is worth to the other negotiators.

The temptation to give things away that are of little value to ourselves is universal. Value everything in the other negotiators' terms. Ask yourself: "What is it worth to them? If they want it, then they value it; and if they value it, what can I get back from them that I value?"

Negotiating is decision making by trading. You TRADE things that are cheaper for you, but valued by the other negotiators, for things that are valued by you, but cheaper for the other negotiators.

## VENUE

Where the negotiations take place is occasionally important to one or both negotiators. A home venue might be advantageous to one of the parties.

- They control the environment.
- They can manipulate the HOSPITALITY.
- They are closer to their coalition members whom they can consult.
- They have access to records, files, and data.
- They are visibly "in charge."

However, one party's advantage is not necessarily another party's disadvantage.

- They cannot walk out of their own premises.
- They cannot claim to have AUTHORITY if the people with the alleged authority are nearby.

- Any failures in the services to the negotiation, or any embarrassments, are more likely to undermine the composure of the hosts than the guests.

When negotiating at the client's premises there is the problem of the security of your recess rooms and communications with your head office. If premature disclosure of your views on the situation is likely to undermine your position, you have fewer remedies on their home ground than you do on yours.

In dictatorships there are no neutral venues, and you can take it for granted that surveillance goes on irrespective of your status (they spy on each other, so what is so special about you?).

What are you looking for in an ideal venue?

- Good-sized negotiating room with space to walk about and work in comfort
- Comfortable furniture, lighting, and ventilation
- Recess rooms for each team, with direct-dial and secure telephones and access to a fax
- Discreet venue staff who go about their work quietly and do not interfere in events
- Everything cleaned and tidied up during breaks, and all refreshments replenished regularly

### VULNERABILITY

Ask yourself where you are vulnerable in a business situation. It might help you to protect your flanks from surprises. For example:

- A short-term lease leaves you vulnerable to a notice to vacate when it is least convenient.
- A long-term lease might constrain you when you see better opportunities elsewhere.

These considerations prompt you to cover your vulnerability in your **PROPOSAL**.

- Management is vulnerable just before an order surge arrives: the employees might take advantage of the pressure to extract concessions.
- An absent partner is vulnerable to decisions made without him or her.
- A supplier is vulnerable to competition offering similar lines.
- We are all vulnerable to accidents.

Thinking about vulnerabilities is productive if it produces constructive measures to avert being ambushed when least expected.

## WAKING UP THE DEAD

A risky intervention ploy. Faced with determined negotiators and not making much progress, you are tempted
to try to explore differences of view on their team. You
invite a member of the other team who has remained
silent throughout the session to comment:

- What do you think, Mr. Sujamo?
- Have you any suggestions about how to break this
  impasse, Ms. Allbright?

You are taking a **RISK**. The other negotiators might
resent your interference and retaliate by stiffening their
position. If the team is disciplined, you are unlikely to
succeed.

## WALKOUT

It does not always work. They do not come running
after you; they leave you to stew.

- Are you walking out to signal total disapproval of
  something they have said, suggested, done, or implied?
- Can you demonstrate disapproval in some other way?
- Why not tell them what you feel?
- What do you do when you are faced with a walkout
  by the other negotiators?

As a pressure ploy it lacks a focus because it is not
clear what the other negotiators are meant to do when
you walk out. The other team might believe that you
are serious about your stance and accommodate you,
but they might also regard you as unstable.

If it is a **COLLECTIVE BARGAINING** dispute, a diplomatic problem, or a spousal argument, the walkout might bring things to a head, though not necessarily in the way you intended (perhaps they wanted you to strike, to **DEADLOCK**, to abandon the matrimonial home).

How do you recommence negotiations after a walkout unless you specify when you will be back? Why not lower the temperature or significance of the walkout by calling for an **ADJOURNMENT**, even an abrupt one to "cool off," to "think about things," to seek advice, and so on. It is much easier to resume negotiations after an adjournment than after a walkout.

### "We should have been told"

A disavowal-of-responsibility ploy.

You have exceeded an agreed-on budget and want an additional payment for the extra work you have done. Your clients deny responsibility because they "should have been told" before you incurred the extra expenses. As you did not tell them, they refuse to pay, no matter that the additional work was necessary. You are stuck with the cost.

Try to negotiate an official order system under which all variations to the contract must be authorized by a named official if payment is to be made, and in return, if an official variation order is made, the client guarantees payment of the extra costs.

*Counter:* Always tell clients when extra work is required and do nothing until they agree. If the roof collapses before they agree, tell them that *you* "should have been told" that you had a blank check to do whatever was necessary.

### "What do you know?"

A long-shot ploy to elicit information.

The other negotiators open by asking you how much you know about the issues. You tell them. They find out more about your knowledge of the details than perhaps you intended to let them know at this stage. Your selection and presentation of detail also signals your PRIORITIES.

*Counter:* "Not a lot. Perhaps you could go over the issues for me?"

### What if?

QUESTIONS to elucidate potential negotiable issues. Useful when faced with DEADLOCK. It helps to explore possible solutions to the deadlock.

**Q:** What if we were to consider delaying the payment deadlines, would that help you with your budgeting?

Also useful when faced with a proposition that may look all right but against which you have no criteria to judge it.

**Q:** What if you make $200,000 instead of $50,000 in the first year? What larger share would I get in those circumstances.

What-if questions can be discussed as hypothetical elements of a solution, with no commitments implied or given at the outset. This is a useful technique in BRAINSTORMING.

A checklist of what-if questions drawn up before you negotiate is a useful **PREPARATION** tool.

## Win-win

I win, you win, so we both win. The goal of an effective negotiator (see **NONZERO SUM**).

In negotiating there are four possible outcomes defined in terms of winning or losing.

1. We both win.
2. I win, you lose.
3. I lose, you win.
4. We both lose.

We both lose in a **DEADLOCK**. The time spent negotiating could have been used for something more profitable, and we may experience long-term disagreeable consequences (litigation).

Either of us winning with the other losing is also an unattractive outcome. If I win at your expense (I sell you a failing business as a going concern), I risk destroying my reputation or our relationship. If for any reason you are unhappy with the deal or how we arrived at it, my winning is a Pyrrhic victory. It could cost me dearly later.

The win-win outcome is the most desirable. It gives both of us a stake in the implementation of the **AGREEMENT**. On the basis of our experience, both of us are willing to consider doing more business in future and to pass on our helpful judgments about one another to third parties.

## Yesable proposition

A seller's ploy, based on the momentum generated by buyers saying yes to a series of proposals. If they keep saying yes, they will eventually say yes to the closing proposition (in theory).

**Q:** You do have a problem with copying costs?

**A:** Yes.

**Q:** You accept that the Corex Copier copies more times per cent than any other on the market?

**A:** Yes.

**Q:** You want to start making big savings on copier costs right away?

**A:** Yes.

**Q:** Will you okay this request for a Corex Copier for delivery in 72 hours?

**A:** Yes.

It is not always so easy, but it is likely to be tried on you from time to time.

*Counter:* YES, BUT . . .

## Yes, but . . .

A closing ploy.

"Your offer is acceptable, but for one small point." You meet the point in some way, and then expect agreement. "Fine. But there is this other detail we must settle." If you settle this issue, another one will pop up, and for as many acceptances as you make, they produce "yes, but . . ."

*Counter:* Identify all the reservations, and address them in one package.

Exorcise the "yes, but . . . by retaliating with the "no, but . . .": "I cannot accept movement on this small detail, but if you accept a change in this other point, I am prepared to consider a change in what you are now asking."

### "You win some and you lose some"

Do not underestimate the need to "save face"; it motivates almost everyone. You have put a lot of effort into an issue, argued long and strong for an outcome, perhaps even thrown in the odd THREAT or two, but in the end you realize you cannot get anything like what you want.

What do you do? Press on with the conflict? It is often better from the negotiator's point of view to admit defeat gracefully. Laugh it off:

• Well, Chris, you win some and you lose some, and this is not my winning day.

• That's life. It was worth trying.

## ZERO SUM

Jargon from **GAME THEORY**: what you gain, they lose.

Your **INTERESTS** are diametrically opposed; you are in a state of pure **CONFLICT**.

Some (difficult) negotiations and haggles are zero-sum games (see **NONZERO SUM**). In pure conflict negotiations you perceive your opponent to be trying to gain at your direct expense. There can be no cooperation or collusion between you to find a mutually advantageous solution because all solutions (except your winning) are mutually disadvantageous.

## ZEUTHEN'S CONFLICT AVOIDANCE MODEL

Compares the gains likely to be made by accepting what is on **OFFER** with the **NET** gains likely to be made by conflict (**STRIKE** or **LOCKOUT**).

- There is a range of practicable bargains (the settlement range), and any wage rate within this range is more advantageous to either party than a conflict.

- Outside the settlement range ("the fighting sphere"), compromise is less advantageous than resort to conflict.

- The limits to fighting are given by the expected result of fighting plus or minus the expected fighting costs.

- The workers will not accept a wage rate lower than they could receive by a fight, less the losses they take by going on strike.

- The employers will not pay a wage higher than they could be forced to by a fight, plus the losses they take by contesting a strike.

Zeuthen's model is a two-stage process. The bargainers compare the certain value obtainable from accepting the other party's current offer with the expected value they obtain by holding to their current demand, together with the expected value of a breakdown in the negotiations and mutual resort to conflict. This calculation produces the maximum probability of conflict they are willing to accept in preference to accepting the other side's current offer.

The bargainer whose willingness to accept the RISK of conflict is smallest (the one who is most anxious to avoid conflict) is the one who makes the next concession. If it is the workers' AGENT, the union demand for a wage increase is reduced; if it is the employer, the company's offer of a wage rate is increased.

The size of a bargainer's CONCESSION is determined by how much a particular concession increases the willingness to risk a strike if it is unacceptable to the other side. Naturally, each party endeavors to persuade the other that any move short of the gap between them induces a preference for a strike (raising the apparent "eagerness for a fight" in the perception of their opponent).

Mistaken assessments of the other's eagerness for a fight, or miscaluations of your own net benefits of conflict, lead to a negotiated wage rate above or below what was practicable if the parties had made different assessments. It boils down to an assessment of which of the parties feels strong enough to resort to, or ride out, conflict.